MW00635012

CLAIM THE STAGE!

A Woman's Guide To Speaking Up, Standing Out, and Taking Leadership

Shelly ~
Show up! Speak up! Step up!
♡ Eleni

ELENI KELAKOS

INDIE BOOKS
INTERNATIONAL®

ISBN-13: 978-1-952233-70-8
Library of Congress Control Number: 2021915788

Designed by Joni McPherson, mcphersongraphics.com

INDIE BOOKS INTERNATIONAL, INC®
2424 VISTA WAY, SUITE 316
OCEANSIDE, CA 92054

www.indiebooksintl.com

*This book is dedicated to all the
courageous women who have trusted
me to help them shape and share
their powerful, unique voices.*

CONTENTS

[PREFACE]

If there is one message to take from this book it is this: It's fun to get better.

But don't take my word for it. Top-level performers, such as musicians and actors, welcome the discomfort of growing their skill sets. They do this because they know that mastery will ultimately give them the confidence and the freedom to be fully present in the moment when they step into the spotlight.

Take Emmy-winning actor, playwright, and singer-songwriter Jeff Daniels, who I know through my husband, a talent agent, who books Jeff's concert dates.

Due to the COVID-19 pandemic in 2020, Jeff was forced to make a shift from giving live musical performances to virtual ones. Musing about the learning curve involved in making this shift, Jeff said this during a Q & A session after an online concert: "You get better every night. It's repetition and practice so it becomes second nature... whether it's playing Atticus Finch in *To Kill a Mockingbird* or doing this concert. It's work, but it's great work. It's fun to get better."

Those words, "It's fun to get better," are emblematic of the attitude of a peak performer who understands what it takes to develop mastery in a given area. And what it takes is a willingness to flounder for a while in the murky middle of discomfort between not knowing and knowing.

Jeff is perfectly willing to hang out in the murky middle of discomfort in the name of learning and growth. That willingness was front and center during a brief conversation we had at a party a few years ago. He plunked himself down on a chair next to me, leaned over and said, sotto voce, "I'm going to go to New York and start rehearsals for a Broadway musical."

"Wow!" I said. "That's great!"

"Eleni," he hissed, leaning closer. "It's a Broadway *musical!* I've never done a Broadway *musical!* I'm scared s***less!"

"Then why are you going to do it?" I asked.

"Because," he said, "I've never done a Broadway musical."

As Jeff illustrates, if you want to get good and feel prepared to hit your target, you must be willing to lean into the feeling of vulnerability that comes with not knowing, until you reach a place of knowing. This takes discipline and a commitment to not shirk the work— even if the work makes the butterflies in your stomach soar.

I saw the same level of commitment to doing the work and stepping into the murky middle of discomfort in the name of self-improvement when I was working on a movie called *Bill and Ted's Bogus Journey*. The legendary stand-up comic, George Carlin, was reprising the role of Rufus, the time-traveling mentor to the two title characters. Though he had appeared in several prior films, George was, at the time, more well-versed and comfortable onstage as a comic than on a film set as an actor. As a result, some of his scenes didn't exactly go as the director might have hoped.

When the director told George he needed to reshoot some of his scenes, he was as accommodating as can be. I knew, from the discussions George and I had while he hung out in my trailer, that he was worried about his screen performance, and committed to doing whatever it took to make his scenes the best they could be, even if the process was, at times, awkward and humbling.

Watching him work, I remember thinking, "That's what it takes to master a medium." By not being afraid to do the work he needed to do to improve his performance, George ultimately helped the movie become yet another cult favorite of the Bill and Ted film franchise.

Anne Bogart, Obie-award-winning director, and cofounder of the CITI Company, who directed me in Claire Booth Luce's *The Women* at San Diego Repertory Theater, had that same commitment to mastery. "Could be more," she would say, when critiquing my work in a rehearsal or performance. Anne's words, always delivered with twinkling eyes and a sly smile, pushed me to dig deeper and explore ways to make my performances better—which was just as fun as it was challenging.

My hope is this book helps you have fun as you get better. Because the better you get, the more willing you'll be to step into the spotlight and make your difference.

Eleni Kelakos
January 2021

[CHAPTER 1]

Why Your Voice Matters

I have come to believe, over and over again,
that what is most important to me must be
spoken, made verbal, or shared, even at the
risk of having it bruised and misunderstood.

—AUDRE LORDE, AMERICAN POET (1934-1992)

The scene of my humiliation occurred in a chic boutique in Tel Aviv, Israel, where I was living because of my dad's job as an American Foreign Service Officer. I was thirteen years old.

My mother, Theresa, had amassed a pile of awesome back-to-school clothes for me and deposited them at the checkout counter. The young woman at the cash register was sullen and silent as she rang up our order and stuffed the clothes into a bag.

My mother, five feet, eight and a half inches tall in her stocking feet, pulled back her shoulders and snatched the bag with a flourish. Her eyes flashed in a way I knew meant trouble.

"You have given me terrible service," she said, in a sharp, steely voice that echoed throughout the crowded store. "You didn't greet me, you didn't thank me, and you didn't look at me. But you were perfectly willing to take my money. You were downright rude. If this is how you treat your customers, you have lost my business."

My mother grabbed my hand and pulled me with her out the boutique door. "Sometimes," she said, "you just have to say something. Do you understand what I mean?"

Still engulfed in my fog of humiliation, I gave a noncommittal shrug. Because the truth was, I didn't understand at all. Why couldn't my mother have just paid for the clothing, taken the shopping bag, and left without making such a fuss in such a public place? I just didn't get it.

Nine years passed.

Newly graduated from college, I was visiting Los Angeles, contemplating whether to move to Hollywood to pursue a career as an actress. A supposedly well-meaning relative introduced me to a colleague I'll call Dick, who had high-level contacts in the entertainment industry.

Perching uncomfortably on a spindly chair in an airy, plant-filled, Beverly Hills living room, I listened in discomfort as my relative and his very slimy pal regaled me with stories about how they had gamed the entertainment industry to make their "fortunes," and how they had slept with many well-connected women to gain more visibility.

They thought they were impressing me. Dick, who was old enough to be my father, looked me up and down like I was a choice piece of sirloin. He then leaned forward conspiratorially and said: "I have lots of contacts in the music and film world who can help you get where you want to go a whole lot faster. You've just got to be very friendly to them, if you know what I mean. So, here's my question: If I put my reputation on the line and introduce you to them, how willing are you going to be to do whatever it takes in the name of growing your career?"

"Yeah," my relative chimed in, "What would you be willing to *do?*"

Both Dick and my relative looked expectantly at me, smiles wide.

With flaming cheeks and a pounding heart, I lifted myself off my chair and I raised myself to my full height of six feet. Squaring my shoulders, I looked down at the two men.

"Well, I'll tell you what I'm *not* willing to do," I said, in a growly voice I didn't know I had. "I'm not willing to randomly sleep with somebody in the hopes of advancing my career. And if that hurts my career, I don't give a damn. And shame on you for even asking me."

Their mouths clamped shut, and I sat back down among the palm fronds. I was so done with these guys.

And in that moment, I finally got why my mother spoke her piece to that cashier years before: *Sometimes you just have to say something.* And when you do, danged if it doesn't feel good.

Sometimes you just have to say something.

Whether it's delivering a critical sales pitch, expressing your value in a job interview, crushing a keynote speech at an industry event, holding a healthy boundary when you're in a difficult conversation, or speaking up in a meeting dominated by interrupters, *sometimes you just have to say something.* Because what you know, what you think, and what you have to say matters. And your voice deserves to be heard.

As a professional presence and presentation coach, trainer, and speaker, I've been on a mission for almost two decades to help people, and women in particular, find the words (and the courage) to say what they need to say when they *just have to say something.*

This book is an extension of that mission. It's my hope that my words will encourage women to use their words to make the difference they were born to make.

You Have A Voice

Whether it is quiet, loud, squeaky, commanding, or hesitant, you have a voice.

A voice you use to speak, to shout, to whisper.

A voice that reflects and relays your passions, your perspective, your skill sets, your talents, and your wisdom.

You have a voice. You may still be defining it, strengthening it, or claiming it, but oh, boy, do you ever have a voice!

You also have a choice: The choice to keep your voice (and thus the deliciousness, the power, the potency of your wisdom and perspective) to yourself, or to share it with the world around you.

What are you choosing to do?

Since you were led to read this book, I'm going to guess you're leaning toward the choice of sharing your voice. Which is great. But you know what's even better than leaning in? Diving in. Stepping in with both feet. Flinging your arms wide, opening your mouth even wider, and jumping in willy-nilly, hell-bent on using your voice to make your difference.

If it sounds like I'm pushing you to share your voice, you are dead right. I've written this book to nudge, prod, and shamelessly cajole you into making the choice to share your voice instead of keeping all your goodies to yourself. Why? Because if you don't express your voice, no one will hear it, and the unique wisdom, viewpoint, and contributions only you can offer will be lost to the world, which—considering the chaotic state of the world we live in—would be more than a crying shame: It would be an unmitigated disaster.

The fact is our battered, beleaguered world needs everything you are and everything you have to offer. It needs your distinctly female wisdom, perspective, and light. It needs you to raise your voice to levels that literally and figuratively can be heard (and not ignored) on stages large and small, in corporate boardrooms, and in the hallowed halls where the political decisions that shape our lives are made.

The way I see it, too many women have been lurking in the wings for far too long. It's time to fling off our cloaks of invisibility, step boldly into the spotlight, and claim the stage.

A Working Definition Of Claim The Stage

In my career I have been on stage as a working actor in New York and regional theater, in Hollywood film and television, and performing as an award-winning singer/songwriter. I have shared the stage with notables such as James Earl Jones, Mariel Hemingway, and Keanu Reeves.

For the past twenty years as a presentation coach my passion has been to help women claim the stage.

So, what exactly is meant by claim the stage?

To claim the stage means *to step fully, vigorously, intentionally, and wholeheartedly into the spotlight in order to share your gifts, wisdom, and perspective with others.* It means laying claim to your implicit right to be in the spotlight and bring your talents to bear in the moment at hand.

Actors, musicians, athletes, speakers, and politicians all claim the stage (or the arena, or the playing field) in one way or another. So do executives, business leaders, and any person who wants to share what they know and be of influence with an audience of one or many.

For the professional women I coach and train, claiming the stage can take many forms, including:

- Finding the courage to speak up and be heard more frequently and confidently in critical meetings.

- Giving an effective and impactful keynote speech at a prestigious conference.

- Asking for a raise or promotion, or interviewing for a new position, without backing off or downplaying their experience and worth.

While it's important to define what claiming the stage *is*, it's equally important to define what it *isn't*: playing small and hiding from opportunities to step up, speak up, and show up when your voice and your perspective could make a difference.

Women: Hardwired For Nurturing, Not Leadership

That said, many contend it is only natural that women take a secondary position when it comes to claiming the stage. They believe that women's voices are best used to exhort others into action and leadership, and that a woman's place is in the wings, supporting others in the spotlight. They point out that women are valued and encouraged for their contributions as important members of the team, rather than leaders of the team. Their thinking is like this: You don't need to be a Supreme Court justice, you can just clerk for one.

When I reflect on this perspective, I think of my mother, Theresa. Though Ma was a gifted visual artist, she treated her art as a hobby. Instead, she focused primarily on her role as the wife of a career foreign service officer (my father, Michael). When I was growing up it was clear to me that, as my Dad's job moved us from Washington D.C. to Paris, Rome, and Israel, my mother had a job too: Helping my dad look good in his important career as a diplomat on the world stage.

Lovely, charming, the consummate hostess and conversationalist, Ma organized cocktail parties and dinners with VIPs, fretted over seating charts, and methodically helped Daddy prepare for those parties by quizzing him on the names of the wives and children of the men who would be attending these parties. Dressed to the nines, she dutifully went out on the town on my father's arm to swanky diplomatic events, always his champion.

As a child, I remember finding a book in her bedside drawer (okay, I was snooping) called something like *The Foreign Service Wife*, issued by the United States State Department and chock-full of tips and tools to help women like my mother understand social protocol as the partner of a professional diplomat. The book emphasized the importance of my mother's presence in my father's public life as his helpmate and advocate. At the time (the 1960s) it was tacitly understood that a capable, charming woman could greatly enhance a foreign service officer's career and even help positively affect the reputation of the United States of America.

In an article by the American Foreign Service Association called "Partners in the Foreign Service: Foreign Service Wives a Century Ago," a longtime diplomat named Willard Baulac is quoted as saying, "I know of no field in which a wife can be more helpful."[1] My mother was certainly helpful, nurturing important business relationships that supported my father's work through her efforts as a charming, capable hostess.

Many say it's common knowledge that women's brains are hardwired to nurture and be the "person behind the person," as my mother so ably was. They explain it like this: In prehistoric times, when Joe and Josie Caveman were alive, they each had very-well-defined societal roles commensurate with their gender roles and supported by their developing brains.[2]

Joe Caveman, who was bigger and stronger (and, no doubt, hairier) focused on hunting and providing food and protection for Josie and the kids. His brain helped him in these tasks by boasting superior spatial skills and higher levels of testosterone, which could account for a higher level of competitiveness and confidence. Josie's job, on the other hand, was to hang around the cave and keep the kids healthy, fed, and alive.

To do that, she had to nurture functional relationships within her family and her cave community. Helping her in her mission to create those strong relational bonds were the "language centers" of her brain, built from the get-go to be stronger in girls than boys and determined to be 30 percent larger than in a man's brain. Nurturing her relationship with Joe was especially important. Because if Joe abandoned her, it would mean no more mastodon meat, and potential starvation for Josie and her children. Essentially, Joe and Josie Caveman's brains developed in ways that strengthened and supported their individual roles as both providers (aka leaders in the outside world) and nurturers (aka cave-bound supporters of leaders).

Eons later, these hardwired differences in men's and women's brains continue to influence the way they operate in the world. Which is why many people continue to believe that women's place is to nurture and be in positions of strong support, while men's place is to step into the spotlight and lead. As a supporter of President Trump expressed during the 2020 United States presidential election when asked about the possibility of a woman leading the country, "When I think of president, I think of a man."

Hold On A Sec: It's Not Just Nature. It's Nurture, Too.

The people who point to research suggesting that women's brains are simply hardwired to nurture are forgetting an important factor: socialization. Explicitly or implicitly, women have been socialized into believing that, to use a baseball metaphor, their place is in the stands rooting for the players, not on the field pitching the ball. The concept that a women's place is in the cave, or home, as it were (as opposed to the House of Representatives or the Senate), has been neatly served up over the centuries in literature and other forms too numerous to count.

It shows up in writing, for example, as early as the seventh century B.C. in Homer's *Odysseus*, the epic tale of the trials and tribulations its hero, King Odysseus, experienced trying to get home to his wife, Penelope, and son, Telemachus, after the Trojan War. When Penelope attempts to tell her son to stop his musician pals from playing a tune she finds depressing, Telemachus tells his mom to "go back up into your quarters, and take up your own work, the loom and the distaff… speech will be the business of men." As Mary Beard, bestselling author and professor of classics at the University of Cambridge, writes in her book *Women and Power: A Manifesto*, this passage from Odysseus is the "…first recorded example of a man telling a woman to 'shut up'" and to refrain from sharing her voice in public.[3]

More early written evidence of the notion that a woman's place is not in the public sphere can be found in the 467 B.C. play *Seven*

Against Thebes by the Greek dramatist Aeschylus. "Let women stay at home and hold their peace," he wrote.

Furthering women's tendency to shut up, play small, and stay hidden in the shadows are the injunctions they've grown up with that keep them feeling uncomfortable about or unworthy of standing out and speaking up. Many women—especially those born before the 1970s, when the women's rights movement came into roaring existence—grew up with fathers who worked and mothers who kept house and raised the children, underscoring the belief that men are leaders and women are followers.

Everywhere women turned, they were informed that their strength lay in being keepers of the emotional and relational flame. "Behind every great man is a great woman," went a much-quoted proverb. (It has since, by the way, been updated to read "Behind every great man is a great woman rolling her eyes.")

Now, I certainly don't want to diminish the incredible contribution to society that women have made, and continue to make, by harnessing their hardwiring and socialization to nurture others. There is, after all, a reason why male professional football players often wave into the camera and say, "Hi, Mom!" when interviewed after the game. But I do believe that it would be downright ridiculous (not to mention a notion as antiquated as the requirement that women only wear dresses and skirts) to think we are not capable of much beyond holding families together or championing a partner's rise to success. Evidence abounds pointing to the reality that more women than ever are showing up, speaking up, and stepping up in the greater world in positions of influence.

In many respects, we are in a golden age of women, an era where women have more opportunities than ever to share their voice, own their power, and make their difference in the public sphere, should they so choose.

Women Are Claiming Their Power And Claiming The Stage

There is no denying that more women than ever are sharing their words and wisdom in places that have not always been welcoming to them. All you have to do is look around your community, and the greater world, to find evidence of women's determination to be seen, heard, and celebrated.

For example, in the United States more women than ever are starting businesses of their own. A 2019 State of Women-Owned Businesses Report commissioned by American Express determined that the number of women-owned businesses increased 21 percent from 2015 to 2019, while all businesses increased only 9 percent. Furthermore, total employment by women-owned businesses rose 8 percent, while for all other businesses the increase was only 1.8 percent.[4]

Women Have The Potential And The Ability. But What About The Confidence?

The women who approach me for leadership or public speaking coaching don't suffer from a lack of talent, potential, and ability—far from it. And they don't suffer from a lack of desire to be seen, heard, and respected. What they suffer from is a frustrating, sometimes crippling lack of confidence around their ability, or even their right, to step into the spotlight and into greater leadership.

It was this issue of confidence (or lack of it) expressed by so many of the women I work with that catalyzed this book. I really wanted to understand why it was that in our initial conversation so many women expressed a variant of the statement, "I want to become more confident." And I wanted to know how lack of confidence (or greater confidence) might affect their leadership presence and ability to effectively manage spotlight moments such as presentations, difficult conversations, and job interviews.

As suggested by my proprietary research (two surveys completed by over one hundred professional women, further details of which you can find in my *Claim the Stage! Workbook*), women often express frustration at their inability to compete with the men in their organizations, and the inherent advantages (and sense of confidence) their male counterparts seemed to enjoy. As one African American woman I coached expressed to me, "I wish I could wake up every morning and feel as capable and entitled to success as the most mediocre white man must feel every day of his life."

In my work, confidence, leadership presence, and presentation skills are all interconnected. *Practice builds confidence, confidence builds presence, and presence is power.* If you want to shine in a spotlight moment, you need to be able to build up your confidence, which will build up your presence, which will build up your ability to claim the stage. Because the more willing and able you are to bring yourself fully to a moment where people are watching and the stakes are high, the more you can be of influence.

The more people you can reach with your words, the more influence you can have. To that end, I make my coaching clients raise their right hand and swear that they will say yes to as many public speaking engagements as possible. I figure that the more women step onto the speaking platform and share their knowledge and perspective, the more accustomed audiences will become to seeing and hearing women speakers. And by that I also mean literally becoming accustomed to the sound and tone of women's voices (which are typically higher in pitch than men, and often pejoratively defined as shrill and deemed somehow less authoritative).

As past United States presidential candidate, first lady, and Secretary of State Hillary Clinton wrote in her book *What Happened*, "Other women will run for President, and they will be women, and they will have women's voices. Maybe that will be less unusual by then."[5]

Or as Christopher Moore, associate professor of sociology at Lakeland College, is quoted as saying in an article in *Pacific Standard* by Abigail Lambert titled "Could Hillary Clinton's Voice Cost Her the White House?": "I think the more people we have with feminine voices in positions of leadership, the more sounding like a leader is going to be less gendered."[6]

Silence Is Not Necessarily Golden

Whether you want to step onto larger stages, or share your voice more in meetings or conversations, one thing is certain: Your voice cannot be shared if you choose to silence it. As Anasuya Sengupta, an Indian author and activist penned in her poem, *Silence*, "Too many women in too many countries speak the same language—of silence." Silence is not necessarily golden (except when your newborn finally falls asleep, or you've just made an important point in your presentation and want to give your audience a chance to let it sink in, or you want to honor someone by listening well before you respond). Staying silent, hovering in the wings, and watching others shine in the spotlight will not advance your cause, sell your ideas or products, or give you the opportunity to move hearts and souls toward better, more positive outcomes.

Women's voices should indeed be heard. They have been silenced for too long. And women certainly don't need to add to that by silencing themselves.

I will say it again, and again, and again, probably to my dying day: You are worthy of embracing who you are and sharing your unique voice. The world needs your voice, ringing out clearly without apology. Whether you choose to share it in corporate boardrooms, in the halls of justice, or in government office, the world needs your voice. Whether you choose to share it by speaking up and out in difficult conversations, weighing in on life-changing legislation, or sharing big ideas in a business pitch or podcast, the world needs your voice.

Which, again, is why I wrote this book. And why, I assume, you are sitting there reading it.

There are seven phases of the Claim the Stage Cycle. Moving through these phases will help you find, define, and share your voice. You'll ultimately learn tools and techniques to help amp up your confidence, steady your resolve (and your nerves), and prepare you to shine in the spotlight moments that can define your life and your career.

You can claim the stage and do and say what matters when it matters. Because your voice matters. And so do you.

CHAPTER 2

The Seven Phases Of The Claim The Stage Cycle

In all things, there is a law of cycles.

—TACITUS, ROMAN HISTORIAN, 56-120 CE

The year was 2018, and I was standing in my Ann Arbor office, brainstorming and arranging the elements of a new keynote speech onto a large whiteboard. It was tough going. Every time I tried to nudge the presentation into shape, the script reared up, thumbed its nose at me, and skittered off in another direction.

As a professional speaker, trainer, and coach, I'd spent countless hours putting together speeches and presentations for myself and my clients. And I recognized the messy, maddening, and exhilarating phase of the speech writing process I was in.

"Ah! The creative muse," I thought. *"There's no sense trying to muscle it to the mat. It's going to take me where it wants to take me and tell me what it needs to be. I just have to hang in there and let it reveal itself to me."*

And so I pulled back for a moment, as I've learned to do in situations like these, and just let my mind drift.

I knew the intention of the keynote was to inspire people (and women in particular) to find the courage to drop their coat of invisibility and step into the spotlight as speakers and leaders.

I knew I had been doing this work with my clients in coaching session after coaching session for years and years.

And I knew there was an inherent process to the work I was engaging in with the clients I was coaching. It seemed like this process wanted to reveal itself and become a part of my keynote, even as I struggled to name it and frame it.

"What are the elements of the arc of the work my sessions take?" I wondered. *"And where does that arc begin?"*

I thought about the first phone calls or get-to-know-you Zoom meetings with potential clients, and our first formal sessions. What did they have in common?

"My clients start by taking stock of what's working and not working for them," I thought.

Take stock. Acknowledge what is so, warts and all. This is the first phase of the process.

I wrote that on my gigantic whiteboard.

Where do I take my clients next in our work together? The answer came quickly: *I have them take ownership of what's stopping them.*

Take ownership. Don't play the blame game. That was the second phase of the process. I quickly wrote it down on my whiteboard.

Now I was on a roll. The other phases spelled themselves out quickly:

Take Aim. Determine the stage on which you want to shine.

Take Steps. Don't shirk the work you need to do to reach your target.

Take Your Cue. Stop getting ready to get ready, so you don't miss your chance to shine.

Take A Risk. Reveal, don't conceal, so your courage and vulnerability can move others.

I knew I was onto something important, but just to be sure, I thought I ought to run it by the good brain of my fellow speaking colleague and dear pal, Sherene McHenry PhD.

Sherene listened to me while I laid the elements of the process out for her. When I was done, she clapped her hands like a kid.

"Yes, yes, yes!" she said with great glee. "I love it. There's just one thing: You're missing the final phase."

She leaned in conspiratorially. "Take a bow. You forgot take a bow! You've got to celebrate what you've just accomplished, right?"

I leaped from my chair and hugged Sherene. In that moment, the seven phases of a coaching process I knew I'd developed over the years, but had struggled to identify, clicked neatly into place. And the keynote presentation I had been wrestling with eased itself around the bones of that process.

Without a whole lot of effort, I began to layer in the personal story that would snake through my keynote and help it come to life: The story of my own journey through the seven phases of what I now call the Claim the Stage Cycle.

A Funny Thing Happened On My Way To Broadway

When I was twenty-nine years old, I was offered a small role in a Broadway-bound production of *A Funny Thing Happened on the Way to the Forum* starring Mickey Rooney. I turned it down.

Actually, I turned the role down three times. The casting director, who knew my singing voice was strong enough to also understudy one of the lead female roles, badgered me to say yes. Let me explain how I got this this pivotal career decision.

The first thing you ought to know is that I was a born diva. I was that kid who loved to ham it up in front of people.

My mom wrote in my *Baby's Milestones* journal: "Eleni, age two to three. Loves to dance to music. Keeps a tune, although bound to be loud and deep-voiced. Has good rhythm and mimics well. Remembers songs and words well. Good memory. Sizeable repertoire."

She also wrote "Exercises in the sunlight, free of clothing."

I really was a little diva.

Ma often teased me by calling me Tallulah, after Tallulah Bankhead, a legendary 1930s Hollywood/Broadway actress with a larger-than-life personality and a penchant for being oh-so-dramatic. The first time I sang by myself (a rousing rendition of "Froggy Went a-Courtin'" in the talent show at sleepaway camp) I was hooked.

When we were stationed in Israel due to my diplomat dad's job assignment, I got plucked out of my fourth-grade class to be featured in a new bilingual educational television show for kids. Being in front of a camera felt like the most natural thing in the world to me. After that, I got cast in great roles in plays and musicals all the way through high school and college.

I was the lead singer in Windy Mountain, a popular Southern rock and roll band. I sang solos in several prestigious choirs. When I graduated from Brown University and moved to New York City to be an actor and singer, a life on the stage seemed destined for me.

Which is why I expected to be welcomed to Manhattan by a cadre of enthusiastic producers, talent agents, and directors falling all over themselves to hire me and make me a star.

Boy, was I wrong.

It's not that a lot of wonderful things didn't happen. It's just that it was a constant struggle. On top of the fact that I was competing with talented women who'd also been the stars of their hometown productions, I was also auditioning during a time when diversity wasn't celebrated or encouraged. With dark hair, dark eyes, and olive skin that reflected my Greek heritage, I was what the industry then termed "ethnic."

That obstacle, however, paled in comparison to my biggest obstacle: my height. I am six feet tall. Most of the male actors I encountered (including many of the famous ones) were, to put it bluntly, boob high. I lost role after role because of the unspoken (though sometimes candidly spoken) belief that men are supposed to be taller than women. It was infuriating.

I was cast in roles that called for tall, exotic women, which is how I found myself standing on a large, proscenium stage in Pennsylvania dressed as a dominatrix.

For my costume I wore a massive, red, curly wig capped by a Brunhilda helmet tipped with horns, thigh-high leather boots, a metal-studded black bustier, and a bullwhip in my hand. I had been cast as Gymnasia, a fierce Amazonian courtesan, in the Pittsburgh

Civic Light Opera's production of *A Funny Thing Happened on the Way to the Forum*.

The role I was playing was, frankly, a glorified chorus part. Not exactly what all those years of training had prepared me for as an actor.

My sense of desolation hung like a pall. For the run of the show, I felt a whole lot of uns: unseen, unheard, and undervalued.

I also felt *enough is enough*. I knew I needed to make a change.

So, when I was offered the same role of Gymnasia in Broadway-bound production of *A Funny Thing Happened on the Way to the Forum* starring Mickey Rooney, I knew I had to turn it down.

I made a decision: No more bustiers, boots, and bullwhips for me. No more uns. And I meant it.

California, Here I Come

At around this time, I had chosen to move with my then husband to California, to explore the world of film and television. Three things happened in quick succession: my husband and I separated and ultimately divorced; my father passed away from Parkinson's disease; and my dear friend, Lisa Michelson, a talented singer and actress, newly pregnant with her first child, was killed in a shocking car accident.

It was a tremendous amount of loss all at once. And I was devastated.

For solace, I played the guitar I'd been given at Christmas when I was sixteen, and moodily tinkled away at the piano I'd dragged with me all the way from New York City. As bits of song lyrics came to me, I scribbled them down.

Then, early one morning, I woke up with the words and melody to a near complete, original song playing in my head. I had somehow been composing it in my sleep, and it was clearly about my friend Lisa.

The chorus went like this: "Angel on my shoulder, sing your music through me. Angel on my shoulder, sing me sweet melody."

I threw back the covers, rushed to the piano, and finished the song within fifteen minutes. *Holy cow, I had written a song!*

But I didn't stop there. "Angel on My Shoulder" opened the door to what felt like an endless number of songs clamoring to be written. Song ideas just tumbled out, teasing me to catch up with them and flesh them out. I wrote, and wrote, and wrote.

And then I had another dream. In this dream, I woke up surrounded by smoke and flames, in what appeared to be a safe clearing in the middle of my apartment building.

A little gnome-like being peered at me and asked: "Do you want me to go to your apartment and get your things?"

"I do," I replied.

In a moment, he was back, carrying various and sundry items.

"Where's my guitar?" I asked. "Where are the hard copies of my songs?"

"I didn't know you wanted them," he replied.

"Don't you understand?" I said. "My music is my life's work."

And then I woke up, bolt upright, in my bed. "Holy cow," I thought. "I've just declared myself!"

In that moment, I laid claim to my purpose, and to the fullest expression of my gifts and talents. I put myself in charge of my own voice, my own form of expression, through the means of songwriting. I took charge of my life and my work. I held myself accountable. No more blaming others or feeling sorry for myself for where I was.

I took the reins. And dang, did it feel good.

The Lure Of The Open Mic

The songs I was writing felt like acts of love. I wrote them for myself, and performed them for my cat, Cassie, or to the empty room around me. I had no other agenda but to write my songs and sing them to myself.

Until the day my friend, Joe, came over for dinner.

"What's the deal?" he asked, pointing toward my piano, the guitar propped against it, and the crumpled wads of notepaper scattered on the floor.

"I've been writing a few songs," I said, somewhat shyly.

"Well sing one for me," Joe asked.

And I guess I was finally ready to share my songs, because I sat down at the piano and belted one out.

When I was done, I turned around and looked at Joe. He looked… surprised? Mad? It was hard to tell.

"You wrote that?"

I nodded.

"Seriously? Holy crap, you're really good!" Then he stood up, his voice rising with him. "Why are you keeping these songs to yourself?" he asked, rather loudly. "There's a singer-songwriter open mic that happens every month at the Highland Grounds coffeehouse in Hollywood. You need to sign up and go."

While I said I'd think about it, my mind was abuzz with the possibility.

As soon as Joe left, I looked up the coffeehouse and I circled the date of the open mic on my calendar. I had picked my target. I had chosen the stage on which I wanted to shine.

How Do You Get To Carnegie Hall? Practice, Practice, Practice

Now it was time to do what I needed to do to feel ready: practice.

Over the next two weeks, I picked what I considered to be two of my strongest songs, one up-tempo and one ballad, and then practiced them until I could practically perform them in my sleep. I did everything I could to make those songs a part of my being, so that I'd be able to sing and play them without hesitation, even if I happened to be broadsided by a wave of fear.

On the night of the open mic, I felt good and ready. Scared, but good and ready. I got to the coffeehouse early, and there was already a long line of people waiting to sign up. By the time I reached the front of the line, I was number fourteen on the list of performers.

I sat down in an empty chair in a corner, hugged my guitar case to me, and waited.

One by one, people stepped up to the mic and sang two songs. Some of them were just okay. Some of them were pretty good. And a few of them were unbelievably great.

The more I hung around, waiting, and listening, the more I was besieged by self-doubt, in the form of Moe and Schmoe, my little inner naysayers who hissed my worst fears into my head: "You're not ready to do this. Your songs aren't good enough to perform in public."

More than once, I came close to bolting for the door. My stomach clenched as the host stepped to the stage and looked my way:

"Ladies and gentlemen," he said into the microphone. "Let's give a rousing welcome to Eleni Kelakos."

Admittedly, he butchered the pronunciation of my name. But it was my name all the same, my cue to rise to my feet, clutching my guitar, and walk resolutely to the spotlight.

Within three minutes of my performance, the owner of the coffeehouse had offered me an actual, paying gig. A new career was born.

As I walked to my car, with my guitar strapped to my back, I knew I had not only found my voice, I had found the courage to share it with others. And I was as proud of myself as I had ever been.

Plumbing My Story For The Seven Phases

What I didn't know at the time, was that I had also taken myself through the seven phases of the Claim the Stage Cycle. Now, with the help of twenty-twenty hindsight, it's clear as day.

Let's take a moment to think back on my story, pull back the curtain, and see where and when I stepped into each of the seven phases:

First of all, I *took stock* (phase one) by finally being willing to see that where I was (feeling unseen, unheard, underused, wearing a bustier, boots, and snapping a bullwhip) was not where I wanted to be.

After I wrote "Angel on My Shoulder" and began to write song after song, I *took ownership* (phase two) by saying "never again" to the bustier and the boots and the bullwhip and committing myself to actualizing my unique purpose and talents and owning my voice as a singer-songwriter.

When Joe urged me to share my songs at the open mic, I *took aim* (phase three) at the stage on which I wanted to shine.

I then *took steps* (phase four) to be ready for my spotlight moment, rehearsing until I knew my songs cold.

Then I went to the open mic, signed up, and waited for my slot. In spite of self-doubt and fear, I *took my cue* (phase five) and stepped from the wings into the spotlight.

Once on stage, I *took a risk* (phase six) by opening myself up to the moment and to the audience, singing from my heart even though I felt vulnerable and scared.

Afterward, I *took a bow* (phase seven)—literally, as the audience applauded—and acknowledged to myself the pleasure and satisfaction I felt at the work I'd put in to achieve my goal.

Those, in a nutshell, are the seven phases of the Claim the Stage Cycle.

And that, of course, is my story, or, at least one of the stories that reflects one of my many Claim the Stage Cycles. Because once you finish a cycle, there's always another one waiting to take to you to another stage of your life and work.

But enough about me and my story. Let's forge ahead and look at your story-in-the-making.

The chapters that follow will take you deeply into each of the seven phases of the Claim the Stage Cycle.

Are you ready to drop your coat of invisibility and shine in spotlight moments large and small? Are you ready to claim the stage?

Assuming you're nodding a vigorous yes, let's leap in with both feet.

CHAPTER 3

Take Stock

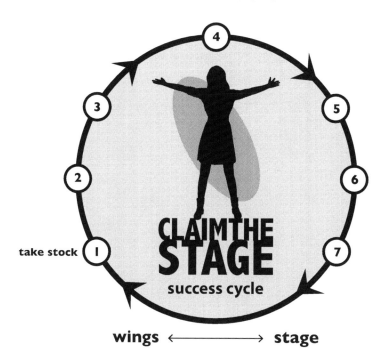

You never find yourself until you face the truth.

—PEARL BAILEY, AMERICAN ACTRESS AND SINGER (1918-1990)

Marina (all stories in this book are true, but most names have been changed for the sake of privacy) was a research professor teaching high-level science at a well-known university. She was the victim of undeserved misfortune. The only woman in her department, Marina was feeling a serious case of the uns: unseen, unheard, and definitely unappreciated.

"Nobody takes me seriously," she said in a teeny, tiny voice. Her voice was so quiet and breathy I had to scoot forward in my chair and ask her to repeat herself.

"Nobody takes me seriously," she said again. "I'm sick of it. I'm sick of feeling overlooked and invisible. I'm sick of not being paid attention to by the students. I'm sick of being talked over and dismissed by my colleagues. Even my family doesn't respect me: They call me Moushka, which means mouse in Russian. *I don't want to be Moushka anymore.*"

When Marina walked through my office doors for our first coaching meeting, I was immediately struck by her physical appearance: She wore a voluminous fringed, knitted coat that dwarfed her small frame. The bangs of her shaggy haircut hung practically to her nose, hiding her expressive eyes. And the clothes she wore—baggy jeans and clogs and a nondescript oversized sweater—made her look more like a haphazardly dressed student than the expert in her field she is.

Marina sunk deeply into my office chair, winding her arms and legs tightly around herself like a pretzel, which only served to make her appear even smaller.

"Marina," I said, "I'm glad you're sick and tired of being perceived as Moushka. If you weren't feeling that strongly, you wouldn't be here. If you weren't finally willing to look at where you are in your life and to think *I'm unhappy! I want more!* you wouldn't be ready to make real, lasting change. So, congratulations! Not only for having the courage to face and feel those icky feelings, but for having picked up the phone and reached out to me for support. Now we can begin the process of helping you step out of the wings and into the spotlight so the world can see and hear what you've got to offer!"

Marina's smile said it all. Relief at my confirmation that what she was experiencing and feeling was a necessary first step toward realizing her potential; and hope that there was indeed a light at the end of the tunnel that she could ultimately reach.

Marina had bravely stepped into the first phase of the Claim the Stage process: *take stock.*

Begin By Taking Stock Of Where You're Stuck

Marina's resolve to make real changes pushed her through a series of challenging coaching sessions that forced her to come face-to-face with the roadblocks that were stopping her. She began to understand that roadblocks (like limiting beliefs and behaviors, or outside circumstances beyond your control) don't stop you—they only slow you down.

Over time, we refashioned Marina's beliefs and behaviors so that she could create a more satisfying and empowered reality. She began to stop hiding and to show up more dynamically and authentically in conversations and lectures, leading out as the smart, capable educator and thought leader she was.

In our meetings, Marina began to look me squarely in the eye, and I no longer struggled to hear her when she spoke. By the time we had completed our sessions, Marina had not only secured a teaching job in another state with a team of colleagues who were more welcoming, respectful, and collegial, she had redefined who she was as a woman, a leader, and even as a (now more empowered) mother of a young daughter.

The thank you note she sent to me said it all: "I am not Moushka anymore."

One Phase Leads To Another

As Marina's story illustrates, the initial take stock phase kicks the Claim the Stage Cycle into motion. This phase involves being brave enough to face up to your uncomfortable reality. It means being willing to acknowledge that circumstances in your life are not what you need, want, or hope for and thinking "enough is enough!" It means allowing yourself to pinpoint and experience painful feelings that you have perhaps been avoiding and recognizing that you don't want to feel those feelings anymore. It's not pretty. It's not easy. But it's what needs to be done if you really want to affect change.

Take stock means taking a good, hard look at your reach and visibility as a leader and asking yourself the following questions:

- How am I feeling stuck and stalled? What essential parts of me are feeling most neglected?

- When (under what circumstances) am I not fully showing up and performing at my peak?

- What feelings am I experiencing that are prompting me to make a change toward a more visible, viable presence at work and in the world?

I typically ask variations of those questions when I have an initial conversation with a potential client. I know they're ready to commit to stepping into phase one of the Claim the Stage process when they respond like this:

Even though I know I have a lot of wisdom and expertise to share, I keep avoiding speaking engagements because of performance anxiety. I'm starting to worry that it's going to limit my chances for promotion.

The team members I lead disregard my directives and suggestions. I feel completely unacknowledged and disrespected.

I was so nervous when I presented the quarterly numbers yesterday that I completely lost my place halfway through. I'm so tired of feeling uncomfortable and unconfident when I give presentations.

You're often nudged into the take stock phase when you feel an inner voice whispering some version of "could be more." You could, for example, be more visible, more clearly understood, more impactful, more seen, more heard, more fulfilled, more respected, more thoroughly utilized, or more influential as a leader. The inner prompt is essentially reminding you that you are not here to play small and to lurk in the wings; you're here to let your unique and necessary voice be heard—fully and without apology—and to take the stage. After a while, this quiet, inner prompt moves from being a gentle nudge to a full-on slap upside your head that you can no longer ignore. That's often when a potential client reaches out to me to begin the coaching process.

Caroline's Quest To Be An Influential Keynote Speaker

Take the case of Caroline, an author and online marketing search engine expert. She had hired me several times to train the members of her tech team to pitch and present more effectively to their clients. I had also worked with her to help manage the anxiety she felt when delivering public presentations (which she tended to avoid). When she reached out to schedule an appointment, I figured we would work on a sales presentation, as usual. I never expected Caroline—a normally shy, introverted woman—to burst through my office door with fire in her eyes.

"I just came back from attending a tech conference," she said, "and there were no women on the main stage. *None.* I can't tell you how *angry* it made me. It's like we're invisible or something. There are so many incredible women in the tech world, and we aren't being given the chance to be seen and heard on large, public platforms. It's *ridiculous*. So that's why I'm here: I want to create a killer keynote presentation and apply to speak at every tech conference I possibly can. I want my voice to be heard."

The lack of women on the speaking platform at the tech conference illuminated the gender inequity at the heart of the tech world, and indirectly made Caroline feel undervalued, unappreciated, and unseen as a woman. Her anger, frustration, and desire to change a limiting status quo was enough to move her up, over, and through her discomfort with public speaking, and to commit to a series of coaching sessions focused on crafting a presentation she could deliver from a larger stage. I was delighted that Caroline had taken such a firm step into the first phase of the Claim the Stage Cycle, and more than happy to support her in her quest. We put together a signature keynote presentation from soup to nuts and shored up the existing tools in her preparation toolkit to help her manage her presentation anxiety; then Caroline went barreling off with great gusto in search of speaking engagements, fueled by the fire in her belly to make her difference.

The key takeaway from Caroline's journey is this: She would never have embarked upon her quest to move from the wings to the stage without first experiencing the discomfort that is inherent in the essential, initial phase of the Claim the Stage Cycle, take stock. This is where it all begins.

Acknowledging What's So When What's So Stinks

When I ask potential clients what propelled them to initially reach out to me, nine out of ten times they'll tell me about a pivotal moment or situation that served to knock the blinders off their eyes and force them to take a hard look at their circumstances.

Often, that moment involved experiencing uncomfortable feelings ("I'm so sad/angry/frustrated/embarrassed/sick-and-tired of being sick-and-tired") combined with feelings of hope and possibility ("I know if I can just get through this, there's so much more that I can do or be.").

Jim Collins, world-renowned business guru and author of the bestselling book *Good to Great*,[7] has a name for this duality of feelings: the Stockdale Paradox.

Collins defined the Stockdale Paradox as "being able to overcome challenges and fulfill your potential by having the discipline to confront the most brutal facts of your current reality, whatever they might be while at the same time, maintaining unwavering faith that you can and will prevail in the end, regardless of difficulties." He named this paradox after James Stockdale, a United States Navy vice admiral and aviator who served in the Vietnam War and endured eight years of imprisonment in North Vietnam, including three years of solitary confinement. Stockdale was a symbol of defiance, organizing the other POWs and refusing to serve as a tool for Vietnamese propaganda. He received the Medal of Honor three years after his release, on March 6, 1976.

When Collins asked Stockdale about how he was able to survive his imprisonment, Stockdale responded by saying, "I never lost faith in the end of the story, I never doubted not only that I would get out, but also that I would prevail in the end and turn the experience into the defining event of my life, which, in retrospect, I would not trade."

Stockdale also explained that the people who didn't make it out of Vietnam were those who were so relentlessly optimistic they weren't willing or able to see their true and difficult reality.

"This is a very important lesson," Stockdale said. "You must never confuse faith that you will prevail in the end—which you can never afford to lose—with the discipline to confront the most brutal facts of your current reality, whatever they might be."

Collins believes that embracing this paradoxical duality is a necessary element for companies (and individuals) to endure tough times. I agree. I also believe that this paradox is a critical part of stepping with resolve into phase one, take stock. The duality exists so you can maintain the realistic focus and momentum needed to move successfully through all seven phases of the Claim the Stage Cycle.

This paradox is at play when, for example, you pull on your favorite jeans and try (and try and try and try) unsuccessfully to zip them up, and finally have the guts to admit, "Crap! I really *have* gained a ton of weight over the past year, and it's making me feel sluggish and awful and not particularly good about myself. But I *know* I can get myself in better shape!"

Like many of you, I've experienced this paradoxical duality whenever I've come to a pivotal crossroads in my life. It occurred in a big way during and after the experience I wrote about in chapter two, when I found myself feeling lots of uns (undervalued, underused, underwhelmed) while playing the one-dimensional, bullwhip-slinging Amazon princess, Gymnasia, in a production of *A Funny Thing Happened on the Way to the Forum*. Though I was seething with frustration at playing a role that relied only on my height and that barely tapped my resources as a singer and actress, I also felt hope and resolve for something better. I felt so hopeful and resolved, in fact, that, as you may recall, when I returned to New York and was offered the same role in a pre-Broadway National Tour of the same play starring Mickey Rooney, I flat-out turned the offer down, not once, but three times. That's how resolved I was, and how willing I was to pay attention to my inner prompt.

Listen To Your Inner Prompt

Sometimes the inner prompt that propels us into the take stock phase is quiet and steely, as was the case with a client who reached out to me when she was passed over for an internal promotion for the second time for a leadership role that should have been rightfully hers.

"I feel overlooked and underappreciated," she said. "And I not only feel hurt, I'm pissed! Worst of all, my confidence has taken a big hit. I need to bolster my confidence so I can apply for and get a better position outside of this company."

Sometimes the inner prompt can be extremely dramatic. Take what happened to media mogul and thought leader Arianna Huffington. In her role as CEO of the *Huffington Post*, Huffington kept up a brutal, breakneck pace— until the day she literally fell asleep on her feet at the office and dropped like a stone, whacking the side of her head on the corner of her desk on her way to the floor.

Recovering at the hospital, she finally came-face-to-face with the brutal reality that she was overworking and not getting nearly enough sleep to sustain her too-busy life. Her injury shifted her entire perspective and launched her firmly into the Claim the Stage Cycle. As a result, she made huge changes to the *Huffington Post* workplace, limiting the hours her team members could work, adding napping stations at the office, and encouraging breaks for mindfulness practice like meditation and yoga.

Her commitment to this change led her to write a bestselling book called *Thrive*[8] that encouraged others to get more sleep and be more mindful on a daily basis. Which prompted her to leave her position at the *Huffington Post* and spearhead a very public movement based on the tenets of her book. And all because she paid attention to the inner prompt that made her face down a reality that desperately needed changing.

Whether your inner prompt to make a change is small or dramatic, it's your responsibility to pay attention to it and, ultimately, to act upon it. It's your responsibility to notice it and honor it when it whispers *"Could be more! You're built for more than this!"* Because when it comes down to it, nobody but you can change your life for the better. And nobody but you can choose to share your voice in a more public and more influential way.

Remember, roadblocks don't stop you, they only slow you down. *So, take stock of where you're stuck.* Because once you do, you can begin to experience some "uns" you'll actually like: Getting unstuck from and unencumbered by a reality that doesn't serve you.

CLAIM THE STAGE!

PHASE ONE:
TAKE STOCK

Face reality. Be willing to take a good, long look at the uncomfortable reality you may be experiencing in your life and work.

Embrace your challenges. Be willing to believe that the challenges you are facing are, as Captain Stockdale put it, something you would not trade because of their ability to help you learn and grow.

Make a list and check it twice. List the uns or disses you're feeling (e.g., unappreciated, unfulfilled, disrespected, etc.) in your life and work. How long have you been feeling them? What triggered you into finally paying attention to them?

Write it down. When and where are you feeling stuck and stalled in your life and work? Don't keep the list in your head—put it down on paper.

Have faith. Do believe that you are capable of experiencing and contributing so much more, despite the challenges and frustrations.

[CHAPTER 4]

Take Ownership

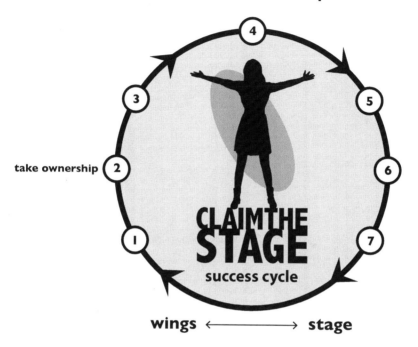

*The tides do not command the ship.
The sailor does.*

—Ogwo David Emenike, Nigerian poet and essayist

Nancy was the refined, reserved head of a large medical department at a prestigious university. She was a capable leader who had worked hard to climb the ladder. But she had a secret shame.

At our first meeting, Nancy explained that she was not only expected to speak at numerous public and private events throughout the school year, but to do so easily and well.

"The problem," she confessed, fidgeting noticeably in her chair, "is that I'm absolutely *terrified of speaking in public.*"

She spoke those words as if she were sharing a dirty, nasty little secret. Sadly, to her it was. Her shame was palpable.

Nancy explained that every time she got up to speak, she was plagued by insecurity and self-doubt.

"Who do you think you are?" she thought to herself. "Who's going to listen to you? Everyone can tell you're nervous. You're *a fraud.*"

The more she paid attention to these limiting beliefs, the more anxious she became. The more anxious she became, the less confident she felt. The less confident she felt, the less inclined she was to speak in public. This was especially true in high-stakes spotlight moments such as giving keynotes at national conferences, facilitating departmental workshops, and speaking at fundraising events.

"My fear is not only stopping me from saying yes to speaking engagements that could promote our department and the school on a larger, wider level," Nancy said. "It's also stopping me from doing some smaller-scale speaking, like volunteering to read a piece of scripture from the pulpit at church or giving a toast at a meal. I want to be able to do those things! I mean, I'm in my fifties, for crying out loud! If not now, when?"

She gave a great big sigh and continued: "I'm tired of the fear always winning. That's why I'm here: I want to fix this problem. Because it's really my problem to fix."

It's my problem to fix! When Nancy uttered those words, she stepped into the second phase of the Claim the Stage Cycle: *take ownership*.

Phase Two: Grab The Reins And Take Ownership

Taking ownership means holding yourself—and not others—accountable for where you are in your life and work. It means willingly taking responsibility for solving whatever issues are holding you back, and not expecting others to solve them for you. It means not just taking a good, long look at your uncomfortable reality, as you did in the first phase, but shifting toward taking a good, long look at what you may be doing to contribute to it through your thoughts, beliefs, and behaviors. Only then can you move forward to a more satisfying reality.

Because Nancy was willing to take ownership of her circumstance, I guided her through what I call the *know thyself* part of our coaching work: thoroughly examining her *blessings* (her unique gifts, abilities, and talents) and her *blocks* (limiting beliefs and behaviors). Nancy's list of limiting beliefs (or what I call *lies that bind*, like "You're not interesting or qualified enough to speak to this group") were extensive and were contributing mightily to limiting behaviors such as avoiding speaking engagements altogether, or mumbling, verbally stumbling, and physically freezing up when she did present.

Because of her diligence, and her commitment to fixing her issues rather than casting blame and doing nothing, Nancy ultimately delivered her presentations with greater confidence and more impact.

Don't Play The Blame Game

As Nancy's story makes clear, the second phase of the Claim the Stage Cycle involves not only accepting responsibility for the beliefs and behaviors that might consciously or unconsciously be keeping you from stepping fully into spotlight moments, but also accepting personal responsibility for making a change for the better. This means letting go of the tendency to blame other people or circumstances outside of yourself for how you may currently be feeling or for the dissatisfying situation in which you might find yourself.

To stop playing the blame game, you must be willing to adopt the mantra "If it is going to be, it is up to me." As transformative speaker, blogger, and coach Hal Elrod writes in his book *The Miracle Morning: The Not-So-Obvious Secret Guaranteed to Transform Your Life (Before 8 am)*, it's about "accepting total responsibility for every aspect of your life and refusing to blame anyone else."[9]

Now, you may be thinking, "But sometimes there really *are* people and things outside myself that prevent me from sharing my voice." And, of course, you're right. My clients are constantly telling me about frustrating, disempowering circumstances, or people (often men) that limit their ability to share their voice, step onto larger stages, or be more visible and influential.

Here are three examples shared in my long-form survey (for more examples please see the *Claim The Stage! Workbook*):

Vita McCabe, MD, MHSA, a cardiothoracic surgery specialist, and former provider chief wellness officer for a seven hospital health system, wrote that, as a woman in a predominantly male field, she has been "silenced during opinion at a tumor board; asked to get coffee at a professional meeting; asked if I was in the wrong room when I was taking the cardiothoracic oral boards examinations."

Sandra, a graphic designer, shared this: "While working at ad agencies, I've run into situations when my designs were better than a male counterpart's designs. However, for the final presentations, my boss had the male designer present his work *and* mine to the client. He gave me the credit, but he was the one who got to talk."

Pamela Lemerand, PhD, an associate college professor and adolescent psychologist, told of a time when a male colleague "took my ideas discussed over lunch and made a presentation to the boss as if the proposal was his idea. He did not share that the ideas were generated through a discussion with me or that it was perhaps a combination of our ideas."

These are examples of systems, circumstances, and people that have genuinely erected legitimate barriers that limit another person's voice or progress. And while it would be easy (and, some would say, justifiable) for the women who cited these incidents to simply point at their perpetrators or circumstances and play the blame game, it's not a particularly effective way to create real, satisfying change. That's because when you play the blame game, you shift responsibility elsewhere instead of taking empowering action on your own behalf.

There is a big difference between recognizing external barriers and limitations, like others being threatened by your ideas, and using them as an excuse to shrug off personal responsibility for frustrating circumstances. "Responsibility is not the same as blame," Elrod explains. "While blame determines who is at fault for something, responsibility determines *who is committed to improving things.*"[10]

I usually can tell a client is playing the blame game when I hear comments like this:

"I've been working at my company for three years, and I've never been asked to give the quarterly reports!"

"My coworker always interrupts me and takes over the conversation when I talk in meetings, so now I just tune out and shut up."

"I'm not trying to become partner because women just don't get promoted to that level at my firm."

Women who play the blame game would rather talk about what's in the way than pull on their big girl panties and do something about it. I know that may sound harsh, but, honestly, if we don't take the reins in our own lives and spearhead the changes that need to occur, who will?

To take ownership doesn't just involve taking responsibility for where you are in your life. It involves taking responsibility for your blessings (the talents, gifts, and abilities you're here to maximize) and blocks (the limiting, subconscious beliefs that drive your limiting behavior).

Meet Moe And Schmoe, Equal Opportunity Naysayers

If you're curious about what your limiting beliefs might be, pay attention to what you're thinking before you step into an ultra-stressful spotlight moment. That's when Moe and Schmoe, your very own set of invisible little nay-saying gremlins, metaphorically hop out of their home in your subconscious mind and pummel you with your lies that bind.

As the keepers of your deepest fears and limiting beliefs, Moe and Schmoe's job is to make you second-guess yourself when eyes are upon you and the stakes are high. They are like little henchmen hired by the brain's amygdala big boss to scare you into taking, or not taking, action based on a perceived threat or fear. ("If you don't pay by Thursday, we're gonna come back and break your legs.")

The amygdala is a part of the brain sometimes referred to as the emotional or irrational brain. It's the part of your brain that takes over—literally hijacking your rational brain—and pushes you into a fight, flight, or freeze response when you're confronted by something potentially life-threatening, such as a fire, or a predator stalking you on a dark night.

If the amygdala could talk, it would probably sound a little like Tony Soprano, the Mafia boss from the HBO series *The Sopranos*—tough and gruff, with a Jersey accent—and it would say something like this:

"Look, lady, I'm basically here to protect you from stuff that could hurt you. Without me, your caveman ancestors would have probably walked straight up to a saber-toothed tiger and gotten eaten, and you and the rest of the human race wouldn't be here today. All I'm doing is looking out for you, okay? And my boys, Moe and Schmoe? Well, I know they can be a little harsh, but they're like an early warning system, a little reminder that if you're not careful, you could get your butt kicked. *Capish?*"

The lies that bind that Moe and Schmoe serve up to you are laden with perceived threats or fears that, left unchecked, could trigger an amygdala hijack that causes behavior that limits you. That's why I typically ask my clients to make an exhaustive list of their lies that bind. Just the simple act of writing them down and looking them in the eye can make them be less triggering.

Here is the dirty dozen, the top twelve lies that bind that I've encountered over two decades of coaching:

1. Nobody takes you seriously.

2. Everyone can tell you're nervous.

3. No one wants to hear what you have to say.

4. You're not qualified to talk about this subject.

5. You're boring, so people won't pay attention.

6. You're going to say the wrong thing and look stupid.

7. Your mind is going to go blank.

8. You're too young to be taken seriously.

9. You're not educated enough.

10. Other people know more about this subject than you do.

11. You don't have charisma like other people do.

12. No matter what you do, you'll never be good enough.

Limiting beliefs like these were pervasive in the replies I received to my long form survey:

"I have a belief that I'm not entertaining enough or funny enough. Getting these two areas worked on would increase my confidence," wrote Lesley Everett, an international expert on personal branding (who is, by the way, quite funny and very entertaining).

"I have this belief that people won't be interested in what I have to say," said a graphic designer in her late fifties. "Changing that would give me the confidence to be more innovative in my design work."

"My go-to [lies that bind] are 'you are too young' and 'others know more than you do,'" wrote Samantha, a health care consultant in her twenties. "If I get caught up in that I do not clearly articulate my message." In the early stages of her career, she struggles to manage and make sense of deep-seated beliefs about how women should communicate, including "Don't come off as a bitch. Do not always speak up early on in your career. And girls are more loveable."

These beliefs reflect the rules around gender and communication that were spoken (or unspoken) in the household she grew up in.

Take Back Your Power With Power Phrases

Moe and Schmoe can do unbelievable damage if you let them. The best way to defang and shut them up is to bravely face down the lies that bind you and reframe each one into a power phrase.

Power phrases are empowering, useful, first-person phrases that you create by going to the core of the lie that binds you and turning it inside out like a sock. For example, "Nobody takes you seriously" might shift into "Because I value my experience and expertise, I take myself seriously and others do, too." Once you've fashioned your power phrases, the idea is to repeat them (or listen to them) enough so that, over time, they become new neural pathways in your subconscious mind, shifting your behavior for the better. Taking my clients through this process is a foundational part of my coaching practice, as is encouraging them to identify, list, and own their blessings.

Use Your Blessings, Or Turn Into Little Miss Cranky-Pants

Your blessings are the talents, gifts, and abilities that are uniquely yours, as well as your unique purpose or what I call your *Soul Role*. I believe with all my heart that you are here on this planet—as a leader and as a woman—to use your blessings fully to fulfill your life's deepest purpose. As I wrote in my book *Touch the Sky: Find Your Voice, Speak Your Truth, Make Your Mark*, "You are not here to play small, you are here to touch the sky!" Finding and sharing your voice without apology and fulfilling your potential involves a commitment to clearly know, celebrate, and use your blessings, rather than letting them languish and fade. When you're not using your blessings in service to what you're here to do, it feels, well, icky—like something is off. It becomes even easier to blame others (or circumstances) for your unease and dissatisfaction.

Take my client, Charlotte, the forty-something, bright, and edgy communications guru of a large business incubator. When she reached out to me, she was feeling, in a word, cranky. As she explained it, she seemed to be ruffling feathers everywhere—sniping at colleagues and bristling at her boss—who told her that her negative attitude was getting in the way of her effectively leading her team.

"I'm pretty sure I just need to find a new job where I'm a better fit," Charlotte said, during our first meeting.

I wasn't as sure as she was that finding a new position was the right and only solution. To figure out what was making Charlotte cranky, I asked her to make a list of her lies that bind, and a list of her blessings. Her list of lies that bind, which I instructed her to write as if Moe and Schmoe were speaking them, included phrases like "You're not as important as everyone else" and "Nobody wants to hear what you have to say," affirming that she felt unheard and unexpressed. When it came to Charlotte's list of blessings, "good writer" was at the top of the list. As she explained, "I'm a professional writer, actually. I freelanced for years, and I love to write. I do some writing as part of my marketing job, like maintaining the company blog and putting out press releases, but it's not really the kind of writing I love."

Charlotte particularly loved to write poems and in-depth magazine articles. It was evident to me that she was longing to write creatively and was feeling deeply unexpressed on a soul level. No wonder she was cranky!

Shift Your Mindset, Shift Your Behavior

To nudge Charlotte into both expressing herself and further owning her blessings, I gave her a series of written homework assignments. First, I asked her to transform her list of lies that bind into a list of power phrases. As an example, I suggested that "Nobody wants to hear what you have to say" could potentially become "I am willing to believe that what I have to say is valuable and worth sharing with others."

Charlotte did what I suggested. The list of power phrases that she brought to me were strong and filled with hope. "Even the act of reading them out loud makes me feel good!" she said.

"Great," I told her, "because you need to marry yourself to these new power phrases. You need to speak them, and think them, and hear them, and see them as much as possible, so they can become new beliefs. Repetition, repetition, repetition is how you create a new belief, a new neural pathway in your brain that leads to new behavior. The more you focus on these new beliefs, the more weeds will grow—metaphorically speaking—on the old, limiting beliefs."

To help Charlotte's power phrases sink deeply into her subconscious mind, I suggested she do the following:

Record her power phrases, reading each one out loud three times before moving on to the next. Then, listen to the recording before falling asleep and right when waking up in the morning, when her brain was most receptive due to an increase in Theta waves. Do this regularly for thirty to sixty days, which is how long it typically takes to create a new habit.

Pick a single power phrase to focus on for thirty days. Make twenty typed copies of this power phrase and tape the copies of the phrase anywhere you might see them (including the side of your nightstand, your bathroom mirror, your car dashboard, your wallet, your desk, and the fridge). Speak the power phrase out loud (or consciously think it) whenever you see it or run across it.

Charlotte followed both suggestions, and began leaning into the new, more useful power phrases. I then gave her one of my favorite coaching assignments: using her list of blessings and power phrases to write a personal manifesto.

Make A Magical Manifesto

A manifesto is a written statement declaring publicly the intentions, motives, or views of the issuer. Relative to the work I do with my clients, a personal manifesto is a soul-stirring, written declaration of self as it relates to the specific focus of our work. It's the result of sitting down with your list of blessings and power phrases, holding your heart wide open to the magical juju of the creative muse, and allowing the pen in your hand to declare on paper who you are and what you are here to do.

Charlotte's half-page manifesto began, "I am a master-crafter of the written word, stirring readers to aliveness through the power of my pen." It was a soulful, viscerally penned declaration of who she was and what she was here to do, and it moved her (and me) to the core. And not only had crafting the manifesto prompted Charlotte to use her writing skills to define and declare herself at the deepest level, it propelled her to dust off a stack of original poems and bring one to share with me. Like her manifesto, the poem was a stunning piece of writing that brought tears to my eyes.

"Write, write, write!" I said.

With the writer in her now officially awake and raring to go, Charlotte began to look for opportunities to write outside of her day job. The more she wrote, the more she remembered how important and necessary writing was to her well-being, and as a conduit of her expression. The more she wrote, the less cranky she was with her colleagues.

The more she wrote, the more time and space she realized she wanted in which to write. Which ultimately led her to leaving her position (on good terms) and finding a part-time position that not only required her to write, but allowed her to work from her own home, giving her the breathing room to pursue freelance writing jobs.

Last I heard, Charlotte had published an article in a major newspaper, dusted off the personal blog she'd abandoned several years before, and was teaching poetry to a group of underserved youth. She'd found her platform of expression, the stage on which she could shine, and was enjoying the satisfaction of letting her voice be fully expressed, shared, and heard. And all because she had chosen to take ownership of her challenges, blocks, and blessings. She never would have done so had she not been willing to embrace—and not ignore—the feedback her boss had given her about her cranky, negative attitude.

Ouch! That Hurts! But Thanks For Telling Me

Taking ownership of our blessings tends to be a lot easier than examining and owning our blocks—particularly when we receive feedback that makes us go "Ouch!"

One of my life and career changing "Ouch! That hurts! But thanks for telling me" moments occurred years ago, soon after I started to give keynote speeches to large audiences on a national level.

After giving an opening keynote at 7:30 a.m. for several hundred restless health care workers at an annual association conference, I left feeling I hadn't connected as well as I'd wanted to with the members of the audience. On the flight home, I began to make a list of reasons why that disconnect might have occurred:

> *It was too early in the morning, and the audience was probably pretty hungover from partying the night before. The audience members were required to be there, so they weren't as receptive as they could have been if they'd come at their own volition. The stage was too small and too far away from my audience. The room was too wide and laid out all wrong. And on top of that, the sound system wasn't that good.*

All the reasons I listed conveniently blamed elements outside of myself—which was certainly easier for me to do than to examine what I might have contributed to the audience disconnect. It wasn't until the event meeting planner kindly gave me the feedback that I might have connected more with the audience if I hadn't referred so much to my notes that I realized the fault lay with me. Though her feedback stung, I was grateful to get it. That single comment changed how I approached giving my presentations, making me a much more effective speaker going forward. Which might never have happened had I stayed stuck in the blame game and been unwilling to hold myself accountable for owning and fixing issues that were mine to begin with.

So, *don't play the blame game.* Embrace the mantra "If it is going to be, it is up to me." Take the reins and *take ownership* of your blessing, your blocks, and the trajectory of your life and work. Once you do, you'll be empowered to move with greater clarity and purpose into the next critical phase of the Claim the Stage Cycle.

CLAIM THE STAGE!

PHASE TWO:
TAKE OWNERSHIP

Be accountable. Grab the reins of your life and take responsibility for the circumstances you can control.

Make a list. Write down all the lies that bind you, the beliefs that stop you from performing at your peak. Write them in the third person, like Moe and Schmoe are hissing them in your ear. Are you willing to believe that you can replace limiting beliefs with new, more empowering beliefs?

Flip the script. Turn each of your lies that bind into a positive, empowering power phrase written in the first person, e.g. "Nobody takes you seriously" might become "Because I take myself seriously, others do, too!" Internalize these new beliefs by speaking or reading them for thirty to sixty days.

Make another list. Write down your blessings. This includes your talents, abilities, gifts, and positive qualities. Are you using your blessings to your advantage? What blessing or gift needs attention and expansion?

Make a manifesto. Look at your list of power phrases and blessings. Then, pick up a pen and paper, and let your subconscious guide you into writing a personal manifesto. When you're done, read it, or record it and listen to it, often.

Here is an example of a personal manifesto (with kind permission from a former client):

A Declaration of Courage + Fluidity

I am a free form. Breath fills my lungs, and my feet feel heavy, grounded on the floor. The floor, the earth reminds me of the fleeting nature of life, and I am embracing and loving this moment.

When I see you in front of me, I am energized by your gaze, your curiosity, and your avid desire for new information. I feel. I am unbound and present to who I am in this moment. I am fortitude, energy, compassion, laughter, hope, and possibility. I am in attendance.

I bring my whole self to this spotlight moment. With ease of movement and effortless poise, story and wit are my compadres. I dance through time responding spontaneously to others, with a twirl of a joke, a sidestep retort.

I am delighted and amused, sense of humor intact. Missteps are like unanticipated moves, adding color, humanity, and character to these moments.

Driven by a desire to be great, I am reasonable, honest, and humble. I am learning, transcending both hopes and fears. I am a work in progress.

Note: You can find more examples of personal manifestos in my Claim The Stage! *Workbook.*

CHAPTER 5

Take Aim

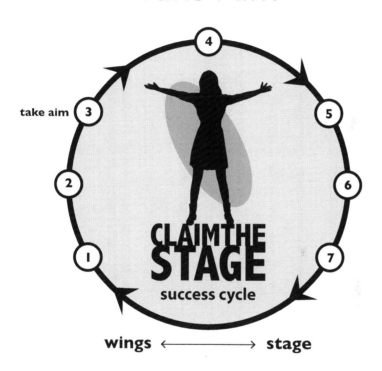

*You cannot hit a target you cannot see, and
you cannot see a target you do not have.*

—ZIG ZIGLAR

Brenda, a warm and witty catering manager for a local restaurant chain, wasn't sure why she was sitting in my office.

"I'm feeling unfulfilled by my work," Brenda began. "But I really don't know what I *want*."

"For now, let's focus on what you *don't* want," I said. "What do you want to stop doing or feeling?"

"That's easy," she said. "I want to feel less restless. I don't want to be tethered to my desk, computer, and phone from nine-to-five. I'm tired of working in the food industry. And I want to stop working for people who don't appreciate how hard I work for them."

"That's a great start," I said. "Now I have another question. What do you love to do? What are you good at, that you wish you could do more of?"

"Well, I love being onstage in front of an audience," Brenda replied. "I'm a bit of an actress, you know? My verbal skills are strong, and I'm great at telling stories. I love to make people laugh. And it makes me happy to be of service to others. If I could find work that could use all those things, that would be *great*."

"Now we're starting to get somewhere," I said. "Let's just keep talking and digging. We'll uncover what you really need and want soon enough!"

As Brenda was walking out the door, I spontaneously handed her a copy of my book *Touch the Sky: Find Your Voice, Speak Your Truth, Make Your Mark*, the companion to my signature keynote presentation, "Touch the Sky."

"Read this," I suggested. "You might see a little bit of yourself in here."

At our next session, Brenda brought the book with her. She'd obviously been reading it, as it was dog-eared and bookmarked.

"So you were an actress and singer-songwriter for years," she said. "And now you're a coach, a trainer, and a speaker. You actually get paid to speak?"

I nodded.

"In front of big audiences?"

I nodded again.

"There is actually such a thing as a career as a paid speaker?"

I nodded vigorously.

"Well, who knew?" she said. "So let me get this straight: You get to dictate your schedule and aren't stuck behind a desk from nine-to-five. You get to perform in front of audiences that stand up and applaud you when you're done. And you get to use the performing chops you love, in work that's of service to others. That sounds like the opposite of what I said I don't want!"

I nodded yet again, now feeling a bit like a bobble-head doll.

"Well," she said, "this might sound crazy, but I know what I want. I want to be a professional speaker like you. Help me figure out what I should talk about. And then help me put together a *killer keynote.*"

And just like that, Brenda stepped into phase three of the Claim the Stage Cycle: *take aim.*

Determine Your Target

Take aim is all about pinpointing and committing to a clear goal or target. Put another way, it's about determining what you *don't* want and getting clarity about what you *do* want, particularly when it comes to your ability and desire to share your voice with greater impact on a larger platform.

That is because you can't get what you want until you know what you want.

Pinpointing a list of factors and conditions she didn't want to reproduce in a potential new position not only gave Brenda something to push off against but something to move toward. Brenda's clarity about what she wanted to accomplish (which, admittedly, came down upon her in one big "aha!" realization that could not be denied, and that I enthusiastically supported) gave us our marching orders. We spent a session or two figuring out what she was qualified to talk about, then another few sessions laying out the framework and the flesh of her first-ever signature keynote presentation. Then we worked on her delivery of that presentation.

As I watched Brenda speak her words and tell her stories, I couldn't help but think: "She was born to do this." It gives me the greatest pleasure to say that, as of this writing, Brenda is making a living as a professional speaker, changing lives through her engaging stories. Whenever I tell her how proud I am of her, she gives me one of her crinkly smiles and says: "It's all your *fault.*"

Because Brenda clearly defined her target, she was able to focus on what she needed to do. By establishing a clear target, she knew exactly where to focus her energies. That's what I call Aim, Ready, Fire.

Know Where You're Heading With Aim, Ready, Fire

While we're accustomed to saying "ready, aim, fire" to describe the sequence of operations to successfully execute a goal or hit a target, I much prefer "aim, ready, fire." You need to know what you're aiming at before you can prepare yourself.

Reinforcing this belief is the fact that potential clients most often contact me to explore coaching when they are at or near the take aim phase. When they do, they typically say things like this:

> "I've just been promoted to a new position, and I need to increase my executive presence so that I can

be seen and heard more effectively when I meet with my CEO."

"I've decided to run for public office, and I need some help getting my stump speech together."

"I need to be able to convey my vision more effectively so I can get more buy-in from my team and be a better leader."

What unifies these statements is that there is a specific target in mind. The target is often a high-stakes, high-stress spotlight moment in which the individual will be required to take the stage with confidence, such as giving a speech or pitching to a prospect.

Sometimes, however, the target is more of a feeling or desired state of being: A more powerful leadership presence when interacting with clients; more confidence when speaking to people in positions of power; or the ability to be relaxed when stepping into media interviews.

The clearer my client is about their target, the more effectively I can help them take aim and hit it. That's why the first question I ask in my initial meeting with a client is this: "What are you hoping to achieve in our work together?"

It's like archery: Without a target, you're just shooting arrows aimlessly. *You've got to see the bullseye before you let your arrows fly.*

For A More Compelling Target, Define The Stakes

Sometimes clients I'm working with need a little added support to help them commit to a target. To do this, I will often ask them two questions that suddenly make their target more compelling: *What's at stake for you if you don't achieve this?* And *what's at stake for you if you do?*

What's at stake—what my clients' stand to gain or lose—is often the very thing that propels my clients to determine a target and seek my help in the first place.

When they contemplate what they stand to lose if they commit to their target, my clients will often share the fears that led them to me:

> *"If I don't step up to the plate and give this presentation, I might not get promoted."*

> *"If I don't go after this job, I might never know what it feels like to achieve my potential."*

> *"If I don't learn to confront and manage my toxic colleague, I'm going to keep being miserable at work."*

The grim reality of what they stand to lose if they don't take aim and commit to their target can be an effective catalyst.

An even better motivator for my clients, however, is determining what they stand to gain if they commit. These responses reflect a deeper sense of purpose and elicit feelings of possibility.

Here's what several of the women who responded to my survey had to say about how their life and work might be affected for the better if they boldly went after their target:

> *"I'd be looked to more as a leader and asked for my opinion more, which would put me at the forefront for future leadership positions."*

> *"It would improve the visibility of my organization and the important work that we do, allowing for even greater change in our community. I can, and want to be, a catalyst for positive change. I believe that is why I am on this earth."*

"It would make me more impactful on stage, and it could skyrocket my speaking business. I could command bigger audiences and more money."

These kinds of affirming, positive feelings help them lift their chin, square their shoulders, and take aim with greater determination.

Create A Vivid Vision Of What's Next

Once my client has determined her target, as well as the stakes surrounding it, I'll often encourage her to write a *vivid vision of what's next*.

A vivid vision of what's next is a clearly delineated description of you successfully achieving your leadership, speaking, or communication target. This written vision is set in the future on a specific date as if you're living it as it unspools in the present. The vision needs to be filled with such richness of detail that, when you arrive at the day and experience the event or goal you've described, you look around and think "Hey! I recognize this!"

Let's say what you're aiming for is giving the opening keynote at your company's annual conference in six months' time. You would write a description of the day of the conference presentation, as if it were unfolding in real time. From that vantage point, you can look back at the steps you took to get there as well as describe in detail what you are doing, moment by moment, as you prepare to claim the stage and step into the spotlight.

The most powerful vision statements also include the feelings you are experiencing. That's because you're often aiming for a different emotional state that's interlaced with the spotlight moment that is your ultimate target.

Feelings are powerful. They are, in fact, more powerful than thoughts, according to Rollin McCraty, PhD, executive vice president and director of research of HeartMath Institute, who says, "The magnetic component of the heart's field…is around one hundred times stronger than that produced by the brain."[11]

A well-crafted vivid vision can make the leadership, communication, or speaking target you're aiming at—the day of the big sales pitch, the morning you give the state of the company address to your team, the day you unveil your first public blog post—even more compelling and attractive.

Sharon's Story: Polishing The Target

Sharon, a dynamic sales professional with decades of experience under her belt, had only been with her company for six months when opportunity knocked. She was asked to take the lead on the most potentially game-changing presentation her tech software company had ever had the opportunity to give: Pitching their services to an internationally known, multimillion-dollar business.

Typically a cool and collected presenter, Sharon was feeling unusually nervous about giving the pitch.

"The stakes are ginormous," she explained. "My boss is relying on me to knock this pitch out of the park. If I can do that, and we land the contract, we'll raise our company profile and attract a whole new level of customer. My boss really believes in me. I don't want to let him down."

"You won't," I assured her. "Let's focus on doing everything possible to shore up your confidence so you bring your A game to the pitch."

Sharon was all in.

For a month leading up to Sharon's presentation, we worked on finessing the delivery of her pitch and PowerPoint slides. Simultaneously, I instructed her to write a vivid vision of her upcoming sales presentation, feeling it might increase her excitement about the target she was aiming at, quiet any reservations, and bolster her confidence.

"Keep it positive and empowering. Make the target you're aiming at come to life in vivid detail. And be sure to include what you're feeling," I directed.

Sharon jumped into the assignment with both feet, creating a document in which she imagined each moment of her important pitch successfully unspooling in front of her. She wrote about how she was feeling as she got dressed the morning of the presentation (*hopeful, ready*), and as she waited to step in front of the client (*relaxed, excited*). She described the way she felt speaking to her audience (*fluid, confident*), and how they were reacting to her (*attentive, engaged*). And she ended her vivid vision with comments from the potential client ("Terrific job!") and praise from her boss ("You nailed it! They were with you the whole way!").

Then she recorded her vision using her phone's microphone app. She listened to her vivid vision every morning and evening for three weeks, without fail. The more she listened to her vivid vision, the more its details imprinted themselves in her subconscious mind, and the more compelling and doable it became.

By the time the day arrived for Sharon to give her pitch, she was not only ready, she was confident that it would pretty much play out the way she'd conceived of it in her vivid vision. Which, sure enough, it did.

"It's like I'd been there before," she explained to me later. "The details of what I was experiencing felt so familiar; now, I was just living them, like I had in my head for weeks."

Sharon's daily commitment to polish her intended target by listening to her recorded vision (combined with the hard work of finessing her presentation) allowed her to fulfill what she'd hoped to accomplish: Positioning her company to the highest level of consideration as a preferred service provider for their dream client. And her boss was thrilled by her performance.

The Positive Power Of Visualization

I became a vision zealot after attending a two-day workshop called "Creating a Vision of Greatness" facilitated by Ann-Arbor, Michigan-based training company ZingTrain.

ZingTrain's visioning model is the very same one that Ari Weinzweig and Paul Saginaw, cofounders of the nationally renowned Zingerman's Delicatessen (which spawned the Zingerman's Community of Businesses, of which ZingTrain is a member) use to define and create what's next for their business.

As Weinzweig, a prolific author, points out in his book *Managing Ourselves*:

> *Whatever I've achieved in my life over the years is largely a testament to the power of visioning... We've spent thirty-plus years envisioning a place that we want to go to work in every day and, for the most part, it's played out as we wrote it. The life that I live, every day, imperfect though it is and will always be, is very much the one that I've envisioned—in writing— for myself...Having worked with our approach to visioning for nearly twenty years now and having*

taught it extensively and intensively for the last ten, I will say with total certainty that it's one of the single most powerful processes I've ever been a part of.[12]

Business owners like Weinzweig are not the only ones who are passionate about the power of visioning. Peak performing athletes, like competitive swimmer Michael Phelps, swear by their use of visualization as a training tool to help them hit their targets. Phelps, the most decorated Olympian athlete of all time, has won a total of twenty-eight medals (twenty-three of them gold), using visualization as a key training component.

Phelps's detailed visualization of the perfect race (and the perfect on-deck preparation for that race) not only helps him win swimming competitions, but is, according to an article by Carmine Gallo in *Forbes*, "a proven, well established technique to achieve peak performance in nearly every endeavor."[13]

The point is this: Writing and internalizing a vivid vision of what's next can make the target you're aiming at more compelling, and help you stay the course.

A Simple Guide To Writing Your Vivid Vision

To guide you through the steps of writing a vivid vision, I'm going to frame my explanation as if you were preparing to speak at a major event (though you could write one that describes any important spotlight moment, like a critical board meeting or job interview).

First things first: Pull out a fresh sheet of paper and a pen. I recommend pen-to-paper versus typing on cyber paper, as it is a more direct line to your subconscious.

Pick a date by which you want this vision to occur. Write it down.

Now imagine your ideal speaking scenario, after you've solved all the issues that are currently holding you back. Write it down in vivid detail, as if it's occurring right now (e.g., It's 10 a.m. on February 14, 2025. I'm waiting to step up to the podium to deliver my presentation at the annual company town hall meeting).

You might want to include the following details:

- The steps you've taken up until that point to prepare for your speaking engagement

- The way you feel as you wait to step up onto the speaking platform

- Who is in the audience

- How it feels to share your words and wisdom with the people in attendance

- How your audience reacts to what you have to say

- How you feel after the presentation is over

Keep it positive and empowering. Don't edit as you go, just let the vision flow onto your sheet of paper.

Then, make your vivid vision of what's next a part of your being by reading it, speaking it out loud, or recording it and listening to it morning and evening, like Sharon did, for as many days as possible prior to your presentation.

Whether you write a vivid vision or get clear about what you *don't* want so you can determine what you *do* want, one thing is certain: The more clearly you define what you're aiming for, the more compelled you'll be to reach it.

So, no more "Ready, Aim, Fire." Instead, think: "Aim, Ready, Fire." Because you've got to see your bullseye before you let your arrows fly.

That said, no matter how glorious, specific, or compelling your target is, you won't reach it without a little (or a lot of) elbow grease. Which is exactly what we're going to focus on in the next chapter.

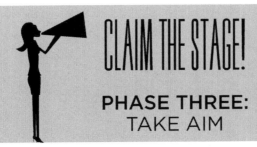

PHASE THREE:
TAKE AIM

Determine what you don't want. Make a list of what you don't want to do, feel, or experience any more in your life and work.

Determine what you do want. Write down what you want to do, feel, or experience more of in your next job, in the next phase or stage of your life or leadership.

Clarify your target. What is the stage on which you want to shine that will give you greater voice and influence?

Determine what's at stake. Write down what you stand to lose and gain by aiming for and hitting that next stage or target.

Write a vivid vision statement. Date it for a specific time in the future. Paint a picture of your desired outcome, including how you want to feel. Fill it with rich, specific details so you will know it when you arrive there. Read it often or record and listen to it until you internalize it.

CHAPTER 6

Take Steps

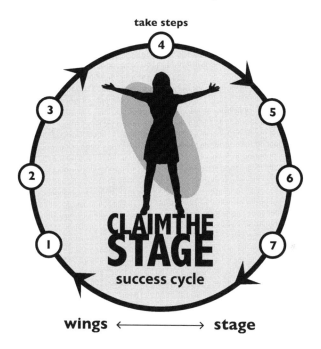

The journey of a thousand miles begins with one step.

—CHINESE PROVERB

Amina was a smart and feisty vice-president of marketing who loved the large corporation she worked for but was feeling restless and underused in her position. "I just want to stretch my wings as a leader," she said, again and again, in our coaching sessions.

Amina was clear about what she wanted: "I'd like to lead a larger team," she declared, "and I want more visibility both inside and outside the organization. I also want a seat at the table at the board level so I can use my voice to impact decision-making."

As if on cue, the most senior level position in public relations suddenly opened in her organization. Amina couldn't wait to tell me about it at our next session.

"It's a perfect fit." she exclaimed "I can practically see myself in the position already. There's just one little problem," she continued, furrowing her brow. "My boss hasn't said a word to me about the job opening. Not a peep. I don't get it. Maybe she doesn't think I'm ready to take on the role?"

"Amina," I asked, "Have you told your boss you'd like to be considered for this role?"

Amina looked horrified. "Well, no, of course not," she replied. "I shouldn't *have* to tell her. She should just *know* this job is perfect for me."

"Your boss isn't a mind-reader," I replied. "You need to not only tell her you're interested in this position, but to convince her you're the best person for it. Why don't you set up a meeting with her to discuss it? Meanwhile, you and I can work on sharpening your talking points so you can be persuasive."

Despite her anxiety about scheduling a meeting to discuss the position with her boss, Amina made the appointment and then prepared for it. She took action, and by doing so she stepped into phase four of the Claim the Stage Cycle: *take steps.*

Phase Four: Take Steps To Boost Your Confidence, Courage, And Skills

Take steps is about doing what is necessary to get you from where you are to where you want to go. To use an expression often quoted by my acting teachers, it's about *doing the work* you need to do to be able to perform at your peak.

This phase can involve all sorts of action, from shoring up existing skills (getting better as a speaker, for instance) to making marketing calls, to asking others for support such as requesting financial donations when running for office or tapping your contacts for employment opportunities.

Amina's first, pivotal step was asking her boss for a meeting. Then she took steps to get ready for the meeting by working with me over the course of a couple of coaching sessions to clarify and strengthen her talking points.

On the day of the meeting with her boss, Amina was nervous but excited, and very ready. I made her promise to call me after the meeting so I could hear how it went; when she did, she was over the moon.

"It couldn't have gone better," she said. "My boss said, 'I don't know why I didn't think of you for the role. You're right, you'd be perfect for it. I'll make sure you're on the short list of candidates and advocate for you in every way.' And you know what else? I was feeling so confident, I went one step further: I reminded my boss that she'd promised me a raise six months ago, which I still hadn't received. Right then and there she called accounting and had them issue a check to me. Can you believe it?"

"Well, actually, I can believe it," I replied. "I'm not remotely surprised at the outcome of your meeting. You earned that outcome by taking the necessary steps: You overcame your discomfort by asking your boss for a meeting, worked diligently with me to prep for that meeting, then showed up at that meeting and let yourself shine. You are proof positive that preparation builds confidence, confidence builds presence and *presence is power*. Good for you!"

Preparation Builds Confidence, Confidence Builds Presence, Presence is Power

There's nothing quite like practice and preparation to boost confidence. And when your confidence is boosted, so is your natural magnetic presence.

No wonder so many of the women answered my survey question "When do you feel most confident?" with some variation of "When I know the subject well and feel most prepared."

Prep By Learning Necessary Skills: Vanessa's Story

Vanessa, a quiet and intense IT professional in her late twenties, was spitting mad. "I'm sick to death of being interrupted by the guys I work with. They talk loud, they talk over me, and I can't get a word in edgewise."

Vanessa went on: "It's especially bad in our weekly meetings with the boss. After a while, I just give up and get quiet. Sometimes I wonder if the boss even notices I'm in the room."

Listening to her rather loud diatribe, I had to smile. "Well, it's not that you don't have anything to say, an inability to express yourself, or the vocal capacity to raise your voice and be heard. You just need to learn how to amp up your willingness and ability to insert yourself into a high-stakes conversation. And you also need to learn to hold clear boundaries when you speak, so those guys know you mean business."

"But I don't like to interrupt," she said, "it's not polite."

"You're not the first woman I've heard speak those words, and you won't be the last," I said. "Frankly, it may not be polite, but you're still going to have to do it. Because most men are quite comfortable interrupting and one-upping each other. In fact, men tend to interrupt women 33 percent more than they interrupt other men.[14] It's called 'manterrupting.' And they're not necessarily going to stop because you don't like it. If it helps, instead of thinking that you're interrupting the interrupters, try thinking of it as firmly and gracefully insinuating yourself into a conversation without letting the moment gallop by. How about practicing a few techniques with me?"

Vanessa was all in, and we spent the rest of the session and the one that followed role-playing conversations in which I actively talked over her and interrupted her midsentence. Vanessa pushed herself to leap in and speak her mind instead of waiting until I made room for her to speak.

She learned how to hold up the flat of her hand and say loudly, firmly, and without apology, "Excuse me, but I haven't finished speaking yet." She practiced sitting up straight, shoulders back, head high, like a queen, taking up more space than usual in her chair. She made sure to speak with enough volume to be easily heard and difficult to ignore. And she practiced speaking in clear, declarative sentences that moved quickly to the point.

To support and augment Vanessa's new *Hey! I'm in the room, pay attention!* behaviors, we worked through the contents of a handout I'd created to go along with my "Stop Playing Small" training. The handout included suggestions on what to *stop* doing and what to *start* doing from a verbal and body language perspective to help others—and especially men—know you mean business. (You can find the "Stop That, Start This" handout in Appendix A.)

When Vanessa had shown signs of having internalizing what I'd taught her, we talked about the need for her to practice her new behaviors outside of my office, and particularly with men.

"Where can you practice this where the stakes are not too high?" I asked.

Vanessa scrunched her face up in thought.

"I know," she said, "I just joined a book club, and it turns out there are no women in the group, just men. At the meetings, I tend to sit back and listen to them talk. I'm thinking that would probably be a good place to try out these techniques."

Vanessa promised she would speak up and show up more fully at the next book club meeting.

At our next session, Vanessa was exultant.

"I'm so proud of myself," she crowed, "I went to my book club meeting and I told the guys 'I'm working on being more actively a part our discussion even if I have to jump in and interrupt. Would you be willing to support me by paying attention when I speak and encouraging me to pipe up if I'm being too quiet?' The guys enthusiastically agreed. And then I did exactly what I said I was going to do: I spoke up, I dared myself to interrupt. It was messy, it was uncomfortable, but I've got to admit it was also *kind of fun*. And I got in a few good points, which the guys acknowledged and appreciated. I *can't wait* to try this out at work."

Vanessa had begun to master a new skill—artfully interrupting—which would ultimately lead her to her goal of speaking up in critical conversations at work. Whether she realized it or not, she mastered that skill the way we master any skill: By moving through the four stages of competence.

Learning Is A Four-Stage Process

Taking steps to becoming masterful at whatever skill you need to improve so you can be ready to claim the stage can be challenging. This is especially true if you are having to learn a skill from scratch, or a skill you're not yet comfortable with, like public speaking. That's because to achieve the highest level of competence with a new skill, you're going to invariably have to move through the four stages of competence:

Unconscious incompetence. In this phase you're not necessarily even aware that there is a skill to be learned, or that you know very little about this skill. To move on to the next phase, you've got to be willing to recognize your own incompetence around this skill, and the value of learning it.

Conscious incompetence. At this stage, you're aware that there is a skill that you don't yet have, and some understanding of how far you've got to go in order to learn it. During this phase, making mistakes is an important part of your learning process (like a baby falling down multiple times in its effort to learn to walk).

Conscious competence. At this level, you have, through practice, become competent at the skill. But you've still got to consciously think about it to execute it.

Unconscious competence. In this final stage, you've practiced so much that your competence has become unconscious. The skill becomes second nature, something you can do automatically without having to think about it. You can even perform the skill while executing other tasks (like driving while drinking a latte, filing your nails, and scolding the kids in the back seat).

Muddling Through The Murky Middle Of Discomfort

Working through the four stages of competence in the name of mastering a skill set that can help you hit your ultimate target will force you to step time and time again into the murky middle of discomfort between not knowing and knowing. This can feel, well, icky (hello, feelings of vulnerability, clumsiness, and ineptitude). Wading bravely into the murky middle of discomfort, in the name of learning and growth, is a critical part of the take steps phase of this process. The more willing and able you are to commit to floundering through the murky middle, the better you'll learn the lesson or the skill set, and the more masterfully you'll be able to perform at your peak on your chosen stage.

Top level performers, such as musicians and actors, welcome the discomfort of stepping into the murky middle in the name of growing their skill sets. They understand that practice makes habit and are willing to put in the time and effort to reach the fourth stage of competence (mastery). They do the work, because they know that mastery will ultimately give them the confidence and the freedom to be fully present in the moment when they take the stage.

Not only did I learn the value of practice and preparation as part of my actor training, I learned it while watching master-level actors at work. Academy-Award-winning actor Sigourney Weaver is a prime example. When, as a newbie actor, I was hired to do stand-in work for Sigourney in the film *Working Girl*, it was whispered around the set just how diligently she had prepared for her role as a tough businesswoman. Sigourney had thoroughly researched the Wall Street investment world and modeled the character she played around real people. I was perpetually impressed by not only how ready she was for every scene, but how open she was to explore the sometimes-challenging suggestions of the director, Mike Nichols. The work she did to prepare paid off big-time: She was nominated for an Academy Award and won a Golden Globe Award for her performance. And all because she didn't shirk the work.

Don't Shirk The Work

Like master-level performers, my most successful coaching and training clients are the kinds of people who don't shirk the work. Because they understand that *success only comes before work in the dictionary*, they're willing to go head-to-head with the hard stuff, instead of avoiding it.

They determine the steps they need to take to claim the stage of their choice, and then they take those steps. It's always clear to me who those clients are, because they're the ones who not only do their homework and are on time for their meetings with me, but who return again and again to the arena, the playing field, the spotlight moments where they're often bloodied and beaten in the name of taking the steps that will help them learn, grow, and ultimately take the stage on which they want to shine. They tell me things like:

> *"I asked my supervisor if I could lead the next stand-up meeting, and she turned me down. I'm going to try again in a couple of weeks."*

> *"Donations for my political campaign are trickling in too slowly. I hate asking for money. But I'm just going to keep putting myself up out there and do it anyway. The more I do it, the easier it gets."*

> *"I'm slowly working my way through my contacts to look for job openings, but no luck yet. But I'm going to keep going until a door opens."*

The clients I work with who eventually hit the targets they are ultimately aiming for understand that the take steps phase is a heads-down, all-in period of focused, determined, disciplined action. They don't make excuses. They don't shirk the work. They just take one step after another, which ultimately pays off in creating lasting change.

If You Don't Ask, You Don't Get

Asking for what you want can be a critical step in moving toward your target. This can be a problem for women, who, according to research, tend not to ask for what they need, are quick to settle for what is offered to them, and often don't consider negotiating on their own behalf—especially compared to their male counterparts.

If you want to take on larger projects, lead the weekly stand-up meeting, get a promotion, or give a breakout session at a national conference, the first step is often going to be to reach out to someone (a boss, a business partner, the HR department, the governing body of an association that decides on conference speakers) to declare your interest, and ask for their support or consideration.

Don't wait to be asked to take that step, just take it. Be the one who takes initiative and does the asking, even it scares the daylights out of you. And then do the work to get yourself good and ready for the opportunity you have catalyzed into being.

Remember:

If you don't do, you won't get.

If you don't ask, you won't receive.

If you don't speak, you won't be heard.

Ask. Don't shirk the work. Because preparation boosts confidence, confidence boosts presence, and presence is the power you need to claim the stage.

PHASE FOUR:
TAKE STEPS

Determine the steps. Pinpoint and list the actions you need to take to ultimately hit your target and claim the stage. This could mean all manner of things, from finding a coach to help you put together a presentation or strengthen your leadership abilities, researching an improvisation class to learn how to be more effective in an unscripted moment, or learning what you need to do to run for political office.

Take the steps. No amount of planning, thinking, or writing about what you need to do will take the place of actually doing it. So do what needs to be done, one step after another, consciously and consistently.

Prepare yourself. Be willing to do the work to get really good in whatever area it is you need to strengthen. Remember, you don't have to go it alone. Reach out to masters for mastery in the area you need to grow or maximize. Tap your friends, family, and professional network for suggestions on who to approach for support. (See my list of suggestions in the Appendix, and in the *Claim The Stage! Workbook*.)

CHAPTER 7

Take Your Cue

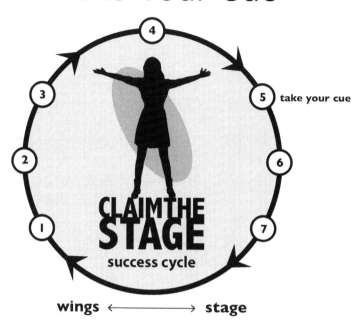

*Hesitation of any kind is a sign of mental decay
in the young, of physical weakness in the old.*

—*THE IMPORTANCE OF BEING EARNEST*, OSCAR WILDE (1854-1900)

Tomeka was frozen on the edge of a big opportunity. "I don't know what to do," she exclaimed.

A stately, forty-something assistant director of development at a business incubator, Tomeka was mulling over a surprise invitation from her boss to interview for his soon-to-be vacated position.

"I just don't know what to do," she repeated, shaking her head, and causing her long, salt-and-pepper dreadlocks to shimmy. "Should I accept the interview or not?"

"I'll tell you why I'm hesitating," she continued. "First of all, my boss told me there are going to be several other people with great credentials interviewing for this job, and they're all from outside of our organization. And they probably have way more direct leadership experience than I do."

"Maybe," I said. "You never know. But you do have years of experience in your field and know the ins and outs of your place of work like someone from the outside never could, which is a real advantage. You have also told me repeatedly that your goal was to take over your boss's position, because you knew he was ultimately planning on moving on and you'd be the most practical choice as his successor. So, what else is making you waffle?"

"Well," Tomeka replied, "this one is really tough for me: My boss very bluntly told me he had hesitated a bit to ask me to interview because he had some doubts about my ability to assume such a visible leadership position. I mean, he's the one who originally sent me to you for leadership coaching, right?"

"That's right," I said. "And we've been working diligently together to up your visibility and confidence as a leader for several months. You've been sharing your voice more and more, and your boss has probably noticed that, or he wouldn't have even bothered to invite you to interview. Anything else?"

Tomeka's voice got very quiet. "What if I get the job and I'm not very good at it. Or if it's not the right thing for me?"

"Well, you won't know until you try, will you?"

We sat in silence for a while, Tomeka twirling a dreadlock in her hands.

"Tomeka," I finally said, "I'm going to be blunt. The hesitations you've shared with me sound more like fears wrapped up in excuses. Let me ask you this: How do you think you'd feel if you didn't step up to this opportunity?"

"Well," Tomeka replied, "the position would certainly stretch me, and there'd be a huge learning curve, and it scares the daylights out of me. But it checks off everything on my list of wants, and it would really push me to step up as a leader. I honestly think I would regret not giving it a shot."

"So what are you going to do?" I asked?

She thought for another minute, then gave me a brave smile: "I guess I'm going to go for it," she replied.

"Good, I said. "Let's get you ready for that interview!"

Tomeka's willingness to ultimately move from hesitation to action by stepping into a high-stakes spotlight moment (that wound up getting her the job) is typical of what occurs in phase five of the Claim the Stage Cycle: *take your cue.*

Take Your Cue: Are You In, Or Are You Out?

In the theater, a cue is something said or done that serves as a signal to an actor or other performer to enter or to begin their speech or performance. It's the trigger for an action to be carried out at a specific time.

Reflecting on those theatrical definitions, *take your cue* means stepping without hesitation from the wings into the spotlight when it's time for you to shine.

A cue tells you the moment has come to stop preparing and start performing. A cue precedes a performance, an utterance, a gesture, an action. For an actor who is waiting in the darkness of the wings to go onstage, the moment of limbo preceding their cue to speak or move is anticipatory, pregnant with possibility.

When the cue occurs, they snap into action. Failure to do so in a timely manner (or to, God forbid, miss their cue altogether, because they were, let's say, dawdling in the dressing room), could have catastrophic consequences for the flow, timing, and overall performance of the show.

Outside of the theater or film world, a cue could represent the moment in a high stakes meeting when you're asked for your opinion, the introduction you're given prior to stepping on stage to give a talk to a group, or before initiating a Zoom call to deliver your sales pitch to a critical prospect. A cue offers you a choice: to stay in the wings, where you have been preparing and waiting, or to move into the spotlight.

The vulnerable, limbo moments that lead up to your cue, when you're "on deck" waiting in the wings (or, let's say, in the reception area in the office of a potential client, or the final moments on the final day of submissions for resumes for your ideal position, or a critical moment in a meeting when you realize you could step in and offer your perspective or opinion) are when Moe and Schmoe, your annoying little nay-saying judgers, are at their friskiest. They leap gleefully onto your shoulders and hiss disempowering thoughts into your ears, like "The audience is never going to pay attention to you" and "You're way too inexperienced to be elected, so why bother announcing your candidacy?"

Moe and Schmoe's mission is to get you to second-guess yourself. They are, in fact, tiny invisible versions of football coaches who call a time-out right as the punter on the opposite team is getting ready to kick the ball over the goalposts. This tactic, which is designed to throw the kicker off his game, has a name: "icing the kicker." That's exactly what Moe and Schmoe are trying to do to you.

Unfortunately, it's at this tender juncture between what is and what could be, between preparing for the show and showtime, in the days or moments before they receive their cue to take the stage, that too many women let Moe and Schmoe get the best of them. They hesitate, take several steps backward and fail to take the cue to move forward.

Marcie's Story: Cold Feet At The Eleventh Hour

After several months of working with me to maximize her leadership presence, Marcie was, at last, being vetted for the position of managing partner in her large firm. Thirty minutes before her fifth and final partnership interview with the most senior partner in the firm, she called me in a panic.

"I'm completely freaked out!" she declared. "This is the scariest interview, with the most important partner! And all I can think of is 'you're not partner material!'"

"Yep, Moe and Schmoe are definitely out in force," I said. "That sure sounds like a lie that binds to me. Here's what I want you to do: Write that phrase down at the top of a blank piece of paper."

Marcie did as I requested.

"Now," I continued, "turn that lie that binds into a positive power phrase. You know the drill."

Marcie quickly scribbled "Because I value my experience and expertise, I'm confident I am partner material."

"Good," I said, "now pretend you're a lawyer in a court of law defending that statement: Find and write down three pieces of evidence that prove each statement is true."

Five minutes later, Marcie was ready to share what she wrote:

"Here's what I've got," she said. "I've been promoted every year in the nine years I've been with this firm. I brought in five million dollars' worth of business in the past two years. And I'm always assigned the toughest clients because my ability to listen with care and empathy makes them feel safe and valued."

"Hey," she said, after a pause, "I *am* partner material!"

I could practically see her grin through the phone lines.

"You certainly are partner material," I agreed. "You've now done the work of convincing yourself that this is so. Once you have convinced yourself of your worth, it's a whole lot easier to convince others. Now go on and take that attitude into your interview!"

Not only did Marcie ace her final interview, she was ultimately offered the partnership she had worked so hard to get. She is now mentoring other women in her firm in hopes that they, too, will find their way into the partner track and be of even greater influence in their work and world. Which is, of course, wonderful.

What's not so wonderful, however, is that for at least ten scary minutes, until I put her through the "convince yourself" exercise that allowed her to recover her perspective and regain a sense of her inherent value, Marcie was willing to believe Moe and Schmoe's cruel lies: that she wasn't good enough to be a name partner in her firm.

Like Tomeka, the assistant director of development you met at the beginning of this chapter, Marcie had fallen into the pitfall of perfection.

When The Three Ps Prevail

The three Ps are the *pitfall of perfection* (needing to be perfect at all costs), the *pitfall of pleasing* (putting others' needs before your own), and the *pitfall of politeness* (avoiding speaking or acting in a way that might offend others or make them like you less, to a fault).

Too many women spend their lives wrestling with, and tipping into one or more of the three Ps, hampering their potential, and limiting their ability to perform at their peak. The three Ps are often at their most treacherous and tempting when your target is within reach. I know when my client is dancing with the three pitfalls and potentially at risk for missing their cue when they make comments like:

> *"I know I'm going to mess this up. I'm just not ready yet."*

> *"I'm worried about what my colleagues/family members might think of me if I do this."*

Being afraid to rock the boat (the pitfall of pleasing), to experience discomfort by advocating for themselves (the pitfall of politeness) or to try and not succeed/risk not being "good enough"(the pitfall of perfection) can make women back off or shrug off a critical target (like a potential job or project) that's not only perfect for them but might give them greater voice, remuneration, and influence.

All three pitfalls are confidence killers. But the pitfall of perfection is particularly problematic when your target is in sight. Especially when it kicks you into obsessively overpreparing, and you get stuck in the loop of getting ready to get ready.

The Pitfall Of Perfection: Stop Getting Ready To Get Ready

The pitfall of perfection can lead to the slippery slope of overpreparation. Once you're sliding down that slope, no amount of preparation feels sufficient: there's always another PowerPoint slide to add to the presentation, another draft of the email to write, another variation of a design to create, another umpteen hours of research to endure.

For those of you who consider perfection a necessity, rather than something to strive for, attaining that perfection can become an exhausting, full-time job. Because no matter how much time you take, effort you make, or preparation you do, it's never enough.

Bob Tewksbury, a former all-star baseball player, current mental skills coach for the San Francisco Giants and the former mental skills coach for the Boston Red Sox 2013 World Series Championship team, has this to say about the elite, peak performing athletes he works with who struggle with the need to be perfect:

> *Those who are obsessed with perfection focus too much on the results and, consequently, have a distorted view of success and see anything short of it as a failure.... Perfectionists establish a pattern of beliefs that involves setting unrealistic goals and expectations, and standards that are impossible to meet. The result? They are guaranteed to never be good enough...* [15]

He also points out that perfectionists tend to have low self-confidence. And in their quest for greater confidence, "they practice more and more, which increases the risk of burnout." [16]

Sound familiar?

Preparation builds confidence. But overpreparation due to the need to be perfect can kill your confidence because it presumes a lack of readiness or worth that can only be conquered by doing, or being, something that is unattainable.

The pitfall of perfection is one that women of all ages and career levels risk teetering into. And it's why, when asked how a lack of confidence shows up for them, 60 percent of my survey respondents replied: "I tend to wait to speak until I feel completely sure of what I want to say." Which very well might mean they speak up too late, or not at all.

Perfectionism and overpreparation can keep women from realizing their potential. That's why it's essential for women to understand the difference between striving toward excellence and needing to be perfect at all costs. Striving toward excellence can help them gain mastery in a skill and prepare them to perform at their peak; it can also leave room for disappointing outcomes and a healthy openness toward trying, failing, and trying again. Needing to be perfect, however, can spin women into procrastination, keep them in a heightened state of anxiety, increase their tendency to second-guess themselves, and stop them from responding to their cue to claim the stage. That's why it's so important to stay healthily self-aware around a tendency to push toward perfection, and to set and honor healthy preparation limits.

Jacinda Arden, prime minister of New Zealand and the world's youngest female world leader, learned to define and honor those preparation limits once she was nominated for office. "There was no time to overprepare," she explained. "...The only choice I had from that day forward was just to be myself."[17] Which meant trusting that who she was and what she chose to do or say was more than enough. Even if she, or it, wasn't perfect.

"Been There, Done That," Says The Recovering Perfectionist

I learned about maintaining reasonable preparation limits the first time I assisted my producer, Doug Messenger, in mixing the recorded tracks to my first album, *I Will Fly*. It became quickly apparent to me that Doug and I could, if we chose, spend a never-ending amount of time tweaking and fixing each song, insisting on making them "perfect." Doug, who shares my inclination to strive toward excellence, and who had spent countless more hours than I producing, mixing, and completing music tracks in his many years in the business, had this to say about the process: "We just have to do our best to come up with a song mix that feels as good as we can get it, and then let it go. If we don't, we'll drive ourselves crazy trying to make it perfect, and never finish this album." He was, of course, right, because, as the saying goes, "perfect is the enemy of done." Taking that approach and holding each other accountable to stay on the healthy side of the preparation line allowed us to finish and release not only that album, but two more. And, in retrospect, when I listen to the songs on the albums we produced, I am more than satisfied with how they came out, even though I know Doug and I could have continued to tweak them endlessly in the studio. I would much rather have finished and released my albums to the world than spent my life getting ready to get ready to finish them.

In order for you to take your cue to claim the stage and reveal your gifts, your perspective, and your big idea to others, you need to stop preparing when it's time to stop preparing. Put another way, *stop getting ready to get ready. When you get your cue, don't think, just do.* Because you can't shine in the spotlight if you're hiding in the wings.

Finding and keeping a healthy line between preparing enough and preparing too much can feel like a never-ending, delicate dance. Nonetheless, it's imperative that you stay vigilant around that line, especially when you're metaphorically waiting in the wings for your cue and within sight of your critical target, because that's when your adrenaline naturally goes into overdrive. And when your adrenaline kicks in, Moe and Schmoe are soon to follow, intent on making you lose perspective, confidence, and focus.

Being unable to manage that kick of adrenaline, and the self-doubt that can accompany it (hello again, Moe and Schmoe), is as threatening to your ability to take your cue and take the stage as overpreparation. To manage that confidence-busting combo of preshow adrenaline and self-defeating anxiety, you need to harness the power of R & R & R: rituals, routines, and repetition.

Manage Preperformance Anxiety And Adrenaline With R & R & R

R & R & R (rituals, routines, and repetition) are activities you engage in regularly when you need to be calm, centered, and present. They are especially valuable in the stressful moments while you're waiting for your cue to take the stage.

R & R & R can keep your mind from slipping into one or more of the three pitfalls; they are acts of self-soothing, akin to sucking your thumb (which we even did in the womb) that can help you find—and keep—center. R & R & R ultimately help you prepare your three presence planes (verbal, physical, and energetic) so you can step into a stressful spotlight moment with greater ease, presence, and focus.

Elements of R & R & R might include:

- Mindfulness breathing (e.g., slowly breathing in and out ten times, while thinking "calm" before each exhalation)

- Speaking or thinking a prayer or invocation ("I ask for guidance and support in finding the right words to be of greatest value to my audience.")

- Writing, speaking, or thinking a power phrase or mantra ("I am relaxed and ready!" "I am powerful and present.")

- Engaging in a specific physical activity designed to both loosen you up and manage your excess adrenaline (e.g., tai chi or qigong, yoga poses, a ritualized series of stretches)

R & R & R can also include holding, wearing, or looking at sacred objects (like a favorite photo of your kids, a ring that your grandmother gave you before she passed away, or a "lucky" pair of socks) to ground you and remind you of what really matters.

Why does it help to engage in R & R & R while you're waiting in the wings for your cue? Because fear (as in your pals Moe and Schmoe) cannot hit a moving target.

Action Trumps Fear

When you are in action, engaging in activities that you can control, fear has a more difficult time sinking its fangs in you. If you are, let's say, intently listening to music, or focusing on tensing and releasing muscle groups in your body, or reciting a mantra out loud or in your head, Moe and Schmoe have a much tougher time getting your attention and derailing you.

One of the best ways to illustrate this point is to share with you the analogy of the elephant in the bazaar, which is the best explanation

I've ever heard about the value of focusing on a mantra (a short, sacred word or phrase like "Om" or "I am calm") while meditating. Imagine a busy marketplace in New Delhi, with a narrow path winding between the colorful stalls of clothing, household items, and food. Plodding down this path is an elephant, with his handler on his back. The elephant is fascinated by the bright objects to its left and right and is tempted to stop every few steps to reach his trunk out to pick one up. To prevent this from happening, the handler gives the elephant a small stick to hold in its trunk. Instead of being distracted by the tempting items in the market stands, the elephant focuses on playing with the stick, allowing his handler to lead him down the path without stopping.

A mantra, or any R & R & R activity you choose to focus on, works like that stick, pulling you into the moment and keeping you from getting distracted by Moe and Schmoe.

Focusing on an activity in your control keeps you from being sucked into fear, or the distraction of self-doubt. Which is why peak performing athletes, actors, and musicians swear by engaging in R & R & R in the moments leading up to the cue to step into the arena.

For example, according to Greg McKeown, the author of the New York Times bestseller *Essentialism: The Disciplined Pursuit of Less*, Olympian Gold Medalist Michael Phelps engages in the same routine at every race.[18] His R & R & R involves, among other things, arriving two hours early, stretching and loosening his body through a series of ritualized swim strokes and laps, putting in his earphones and listening to music (hard core hip-hop, apparently). Ten minutes before the race, he sits alone, his goggles and a towel on empty seats to his left and right. When the race is called, he walks to the starting blocks and does two leg stretches, starting, always, with the left leg. Then, he removes his right earbud. When his name is announced (cue-time!), he takes out his left earbud. He uses his towel to dry the starting block. And then he does the one piece of R & R & R he is famous for: Extending, crossing, and flapping his arms three times so that his hands slap his back. (He even does this signature move when he golfs, right before a critical putt or drive.)

Phelps's R & R & R not only gets him ready to compete, it keeps him from getting distracted by thoughts that could send him spiraling into the three pitfalls right before his cue to leap into the pool in a competitive scenario. His repetitive routines are an essential part of his ability to win big under pressure. As McKeown writes, Phelps's ability to make winning gold medals look easy is "…a testament to the genius of the right routine."

Phelps is one of countless athletes, Olympian and amateur alike, who engage in R & R & R prior to stepping into the arena. For example, one of my clients, a former competitive volleyball player, used to take a cold shower, drink a Red Bull, put her hair up in the same hairstyle (a tight bun), listen to stirring music, and not speak to anyone before a game. As far as she was concerned, this not only helped her feel ready, it helped her play well enough to win.

Athletes are certainly not the only ones who swear by R & R & R. Performing artists, like actors and dancers, do, too.

For instance, Broadway, film and television star, Kristin Chenoweth (*Glee, Wicked*), wouldn't dream of stepping onto a stage without doing vocal warmups (in the bathroom, where the acoustics are good), spraying Vicks up her nose, and uttering a prayer.[19]

Academy Award-nominated actress Christine Lahti taught me about the value of using music as an R & R & R prep tool when, at the start of my career, I worked as her stand-in on the set of the movie *Running On Empty*. Forced to wait for hours to shoot one, brief scene, Christine sat quietly in a corner with her eyes closed, headphones on, portable music player in hand. When the time came for her to shoot the scene, which involved running across a street and bursting into tears, she did it in one brilliant take. Later, I asked Christine how she had managed to be so ready to shoot such an emotional scene after waiting for so long. She pointed to her headphones and said "Music. I listened over and over to the song "I Dreamed a Dream" from *Les Misérables*. It always puts me in a particularly emotional state."

Many of my speaker friends do their own sometimes nutty versions of R & R & R, like exclaiming, "They're going to love me!" before stepping onto the stage. When it comes down to it, there are as many possible variations of R & R & R as there are people. It's just a matter of finding the magical combination of elements that will be effective for you.

Use What Works for You

While Michael Phelps slaps his back like a big-winged bird, that probably won't work for you. Your R & R & R needs to be customized, repeatable, and something you would actually do.

Each of my clients selects specific R & R & R that works best for them. For example:

Tomeka, the client you met at the beginning of this chapter, does a brief mindfulness meditation and mutters mantras before stepping into a spotlight moment.

Another client, an avid golfer, putts a golf ball over and over into a cup, which focuses and grounds him.

Yet another client wears her teeny tiny bodybuilding bikini under her business suit when she goes into important client meetings because it makes her feel powerful.

Still another client makes sure to keep a special water bottle within grabbing distance whenever she steps into a stressful spotlight moment. The bottle is covered in labels featuring soothing and uplifting power phrases ("I am powerful.") and words ("Gratitude," "Relaxed," "Ready"). Reading the words on the water bottle helps her stay focused and centered. A variant of the water bottle as a grounding tool (and one of my all-time favorite bits of R & R & R) was revealed to me years ago by a client who said she calls her bottle of water "Diva juice." "Whenever I feel nervous and want a blast of confidence, I take a sip of my Diva juice!" she said. "It works every time."

And in a survey response that made me laugh out loud, Human Resources trainer Kim Wehrmeister revealed that her favorite way to relieve presentation stress is "listening to heavy metal music, preferably Metallica, at maximum volume in my car on my way there, singing/screaming at the top of my lungs."

As for me, I wouldn't dream of going onstage without warming up my voice and body and doing a speed-through of the opening of my presentation. And I always practice a simple, three-part preparation ritual I call F.B.I. (Foot, Breath, Intention). First, I find the floor with my feet and root myself. Then, I bring my breath into my belly, slowly inhaling and exhaling until I am calm and centered. Finally, I reconnect with my intention (what I am there to do) and step onto the stage.

Pinpoint the R & R & R that works for you and practice it regularly. Use it to help yourself step up and speak up with confidence when your cue comes to take the stage.

Why? Because missing or shirking your cue by second-guessing your readiness or worthiness, overpreparing, or letting Moe and Schmoe broadside you with fear defeats the whole purpose of having a target to aim for and a purpose to honor. No one will hear your words, your wisdom, and your perspective if you let fear or doubt stop you from claiming the stage. As mastermind group facilitator and real estate developer, Katy Fleming, puts it, "It's better to be imperfect than silent."

You can't shine in the spotlight if you hide in the wings. So, *stop getting ready to get ready! When you get your cue, don't think, just do.* Respect the work, time, and effort you've put into preparing yourself by trusting that what you've done is enough. Then center yourself with a little R & R & R and step boldly into your spotlight moment.

CLAIM THE STAGE!

PHASE FIVE:
TAKE YOUR CUE

Stop getting ready to get ready. Be willing to understand and accept that there is a time to engage in preparation, and a time to end it. When the time comes, be willing to step up and take your cue to go claim the stage.

Avoid the three pitfalls. Ask yourself if you're prone to stepping into any or all of the three pitfalls: the pitfall of perfection, the pitfall of politeness, and the pitfall of pleasing. Remember that they can keep you playing small, at the expense of magnifying your unique presence, perspective, and voice.

Embrace excellence, not perfection. Perfection is an impossible state to achieve. Better to reach for excellence by doing the best you can in any given moment and being kind to yourself when things don't go as well as you might have hoped.

Engage in R & R & R. Help yourself stay focused, centered, and ready while you're on deck waiting to take the stage by regularly using rituals, routines, and repetition. Choose and use whatever works for you, including breathing and relaxation techniques, positive self-talk (mutter those mantras and power phrases), sacred objects (a special ring, a lucky charm), and physical activities (like standing for three minutes in a confidence-boosting hands-on-hips, Wonder Woman power pose) that energize and empower you.

Take a Risk

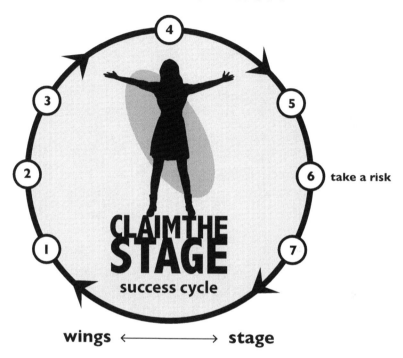

take a risk

*Sure. But that's the fun of it, right? I mean,
you know, we're not here to play it safe.*

—COMEDIC ACTOR JULIA LOUIS-DREYFUS, WHEN ASKED ON NATIONAL
PUBLIC RADIO IF IT WAS A RISK TO PLAY AN UNEXPECTEDLY DRAMATIC
ROLE IN *FORCE MAJEURE*

Holly, a striking and passionate advocate for women's empowerment
in her late thirties, was ready to walk her talk.

"I'm doing my first real keynote to a group of awesome women," she said, in our initial Zoom call. "And I want them to leave feeling like they can do and be anything they can dream of doing or being."

This woman is a force of nature, I thought, and leaped in to help her craft what I knew would be a formidable keynote.

Six weeks and many intense coaching sessions later, we had pulled together a keynote filled not only with Holly's fiery, inspirational spirit, but deeply personal stories that reflected her humanity and vulnerability.

"It's going to be hard to tell this one," Holly said, in reference to a signature story about coming out of the closet as a queer woman in a small, conservative town, and struggling to stand in her power. "But how can I ask my audience to courageously express their voice if I don't courageously express my own?"

One week before the event, Holly texted me to share some really distressing news. It seemed that a man she'd known from a previous job, who had in the past made disparaging remarks about her short-cropped stylish hair, her edgy glasses, and her sexual preference, had begun to suddenly harass her on social media. He'd come across the ad for Holly's upcoming speech and hissed his disapproval of both it and her by emailing her anonymously through her blog and threatening to shoot her in the face with a twelve-gauge shotgun. Most disturbing was his comment that he knew where she'd be speaking in five days so she'd better watch her back.

"We notified the police," Holly said, referring to her equally alarmed wife, "and they're going to keep watch on our house for the next few days, and have a police presence at the event. But I've gotta say, if I was nervous about this speaking gig before, now my anxiety is crazy-high."

Nevertheless, Holly pressed on. "I'm not going to let this guy stop me from getting up on stage and giving this keynote!" she declared.

I admit I fretted and worried about Holly for the next few days, until I received a barrage of texts from her moments after she'd given her speech.

"It's over," she wrote. "I did it! Wow! What a day! I was feeling pumped this morning. But then I was hit with a wave of emotion when I met the police officers at the venue. The way the female officer looked me in the eye and shook my hand—it shook me. And then I had to spend part of the morning trying to shake the feeling of this whole scary incident. It felt like a shadow lurking and like I could burst into tears. Or throw up. I went to the speakers lounge and did a meditation and grounded myself in the energy of safety and of light. And I reminded myself 'this is not about me. I'm just a conduit.' And then, I went out and connected with all the incredible, powerful women and soaked in that light. Here are some pics!"

The images attached to her text brought me instantly to tears: Holly standing like a queen at the podium, wearing a stylish power suit, beaming at the audience as they gave her a rousing, standing ovation. A picture of her hugging her proud, smiling wife. A photo of her with an arm around a grinning policewoman. Triumphant images of a triumphant experience.

There was one more text. "By the way," it said, "I launched my coaching website today, too," she wrote, "and announced it from the stage. It was a huge day for me, and I didn't let that stalker stop me."

Reading Holly's triumphant text, and looking at Holly's pictures, I couldn't have been prouder. It was clear that she had stepped wholeheartedly, with courage and commitment, into the sixth phase of the Claim the Stage Cycle: *take a risk*.

The Sixth Phase: Take a Risk—Reveal, Don't Conceal

Take a risk means being willing to claim the stage with everything you've got. It means stepping into the spotlight, and in the moment as it's unfolding, without reservation, even if it's scary, letting yourself be fully seen and heard. Take a risk means revealing the truth of who you are, what you know, and what you believe. It means letting go of the cloak of invisibility and being willing to be vulnerable, human, and real in front of whoever is watching, no matter what the moment brings. Or as Freddy Miyares, the actor who played Raymond Santana in the Netflix movie *When They See Us*, replied when asked by talk show host Oprah Winfrey how he'd managed to embody his character so compellingly, it's about being "…vulnerable to the circumstances that are present."

My acting teachers called taking the risk to be fully present "showing up." Showing up means bringing your whole, imperfect self to the moment, even if you're worried you might not be liked or you might be rejected. Taking the risk to show up fully and authentically is what claiming the stage is fundamentally all about: being present, being real, being open. It is bringing your best to a spotlight moment, no matter what it brings to you.

While most take-a-risk experiences are not nearly as dramatic as Holly's, they all require the courage to stay open and vulnerable to whatever the moment or situation brings—whether it's joy, fear, awkwardness, or uncertainty.

For example, taking a risk can be finally finding the courage to speak your truth by saying to your boss, "As a PhD with many years of scientific experience, I would prefer it if you would not ask me to order lunch for the team just because I'm the only woman in the group."

It can be telling a colleague who likes to tell blonde jokes in your presence, "As a blonde, and as a woman, I am offended by your jokes. Please stop telling them in my presence."

It can be stepping onto a stage as a political candidate or insinuating yourself into the conversation at a meeting and sharing an opposing or unpopular perspective because you know in your heart this is the right thing to do.

It can be getting in front of your team, your partner, or a colleague and apologizing with all your heart for a decision you made that caused them to suffer financially, emotionally, or otherwise.

It can be allowing your quirky and unique sense of humor to make an appearance during an interview because, when it comes down to it, you want to be employed somewhere where that essential part of you is valued.

Or perhaps a take a risk moment can take the form of revealing your vulnerable self to your employees for the very first time, as it was for my client, Violet.

Violet's Story: The Courage To Reveal

Violet, the impish, fortyish co-owner of a successful employment agency, looked positively anguished when she showed up for our coaching session.

"I cannot for the life of me figure out what story to tell when I deliver my speech to my team at the holiday party," she exclaimed.

"It's a really big moment," she confessed, "because it's the first time I'll be giving the speech and not my business partner. Our employees are going to be shocked! They think of me as a behind-the-scenes cheerleaderish sort of leader, not the kind that steps into the spotlight and gives speeches. But my partner and I agree that having me give the annual speech might help our team members see how much I've matured as a leader since I came on board three years ago."

"Tell me more about what these last three years have been like," I prompted.

"Well, when I was asked to join the company, I was scared to death because both the industry and the level of leadership were new to me," Violet confessed. "I almost didn't do it. But my husband convinced me I'd be good at it. So I said yes, and jumped in. I learned on my feet, made a ton of mistakes. I mean, there were days I thought *I have absolutely no idea what I'm doing!* But, somehow, I muddled through. Three years later, look at where I am! I love my work, and most of all, I love the people I work with. I wouldn't want to work anywhere else, with anyone else!"

"Violet," I said, "that's the kernel of a compelling story. Would you be willing to flesh it out and share it with your team members?"

Violet looked horrified.

"Oh my gosh," she said, "I've never revealed myself that much to them before. Isn't that too personal, too real? And what if I get emotional while I speak? I mean, I'm a crier! Wouldn't that make me look less leader-like and professional?"

I shook my head.

"Violet, I assure you, if you risk being real, you'll build real trust, which builds real relationships with your team members. And if tears come, just let them come. Then, take a breath, pull yourself together, and keep talking."

Though Violet looked doubtful about the whole concept of being so transparent with her team members, she grudgingly agreed to give it a shot. We put together a warm, intimate speech that featured Violet's story. Then I had her practice it until she felt ready for her spotlight moment.

Within an hour after she'd given her speech at the company holiday party, Violet called me, exultant. "I did it, I did it!" she exclaimed, "I shared my story, and it was scary, and emotional, and I even cried a little bit. But when I was done, person after person came up to me to hug me or shake my hand, or to tell me how much they appreciated that I had spoken from my heart so fully to them. It was amazing."

What was even more amazing was how much closer and more committed to her team members Violet felt in the days and months following her speech. And that closeness and commitment was returned by her employees, who now saw Violet differently because of her willingness to take the risk of revealing herself so genuinely and humanly.

Violet now understands that great leaders, like great speakers, are willing to take the risk of being real, and therefore even more relatable, to their audiences of one or many. Because being real builds trust, which builds relationships.

That said, "being real" is not exactly easy. Because "being real" means revealing who you really are and what you really think or feel to people who also have opinions and points of view which may or may not be in alignment with yours. Which is, to say the least, scary as hell. *What will they think of me? What if I'm not good enough?* No wonder too many of us choose to stay hidden under our cloaks of invisibility, looking longingly from the wings at the stage that beckons.

Here's the thing: If you want to be more than a supporting player on the stage that is your life and to touch souls, change lives, and shift perspectives through your words and work, you have to find the courage to drop your coat of invisibility. You must step into the spotlight, and reveal your gifts, your truths, your stories, and your hearts. Like Violet, you must encourage your courage.

Encouraging Everyday Courage

So, what exactly is courage, anyway?

Some say courage is the choice and willingness to confront agony, pain, danger, uncertainty, or intimidation.

Others define it as mental or moral strength to resist opposition, danger, or hardship.

The dictionary definition of *courage* is: "The quality of mind or spirit that enables a person to face difficulty, danger, pain, etc. without fear; bravery."

Reading these definitions makes me think of big acts of bravery, like leading troops into bloody battle or stepping into a burning building to rescue a child. While these are certainly valiant acts of courage, they can feel discouragingly out of reach for most people, especially women. Here's how authors Megan Raphael and Jennifer Byron express that disconnect in their thoughtful book *The Courage Code*:

> *For eons there has been an unspoken language around courage—a Code—that is distinctly masculine. It's*

a Code that defines courage in a singular way…as big, bold acts of valor and victory. In this Code, the synonym for courage is bravery, especially in the face of immediate life-threatening danger. It refers to huge accomplishments, typically physical, such as mountain climbing, sky diving or adventuring in the Australian Outback….Women see how the world views courage, so we say we're not courageous. We compare ourselves to the role models that are touted by the media and we feel we fall far short. As a result, we begin to believe we are not enough—not courageous or bold or valorous enough. We downplay ourselves and our actions.[20]

Since I believe with all my heart that women are inherently worthy and courageous, I'd like to suggest a more doable and accessible definition of courage. It was tweeted by acclaimed thought leader, bestselling author, and sociologist, Dr. Brené Brown, on Valentine's Day, 2018:

"The root of the word courage is *cor*—the Latin word for heart. In one of its earliest forms, the word courage meant 'to speak one's mind by telling all one's heart.' Courage is a heart word."

Is there anything that requires a greater willingness to dare to bare, to risk revealing, to encourage courage than "speaking one's own mind by telling all one's heart?"

On a related note, I disagree with the dictionary definition that says courage must come without fear. Because, as Dr. Brown also says, "you can be both courageous and afraid at the same time," which anyone who has gone into battle, asked for a raise, chosen to disagree with a valuable colleague or client, or said "I love you" for the first time can understand.

My clients continuously engage in small acts of courage as they work their way up toward the larger degree of courage they'll need to shine in their ultimate spotlight moment. For example, I recently had a coaching client tell me with great pride that, in line with the work we were doing together to help her be seen as a more viable, promotable leader, she had made herself do something she typically avoids: Speak up during her company's monthly executive team meeting. "I was scared, but I did it anyway," she said, "and guess what? My comment provoked a question, which I had to answer. It wasn't nearly as awful as I expected! So I'm just going to keep on doing it."

Another client had to exercise her courage muscle every time she visited my office. Not just because she was so utterly terrified of speaking in public that even the idea of meeting with me to work through her fear made her want to run and hide, but because she was also scared of driving anywhere outside of a few familiar blocks in her hometown. For our first few sessions, she had her son drive her the fifty-or-so miles to my office.

One day, she surprised the heck out of me by pulling into my driveway and waving at me from behind the wheel of her car. Her son was nowhere to be seen. "I thought it was time for me to drive here myself," she said, with not a little bit of pride etched on her face. Since courage begets courage, my client's efforts to engage in small, regular acts of courage, like driving herself to my office, and working on her coaching assignments, increased her level of confidence and allowed her to fulfill her ultimate goal: Delivering a short, scripted speech to me, on the small, lit stage in my office, which she did with a minimum of fear and maximum of courage. That's what engaging in one-bite-at-a-time, small acts of courage can do.

Time and again my clients have demonstrated the value of engaging in small acts of everyday courage, like asking a question during a packed lecture, sending their blog post out regularly, or speaking up when they are misunderstood or wronged. ("No, I actually didn't write the memo that prompted the error you're referring to.") The more they engage in these small acts of courage, the more they strengthen their courage muscle, boost their confidence, and prepare themselves for even bigger bolder acts of courage.

For example, if you are considering running for public office, engaging in small acts of courage, like reaching out to local politicians for insight into the logistics of a political campaign, can strengthen your ability to take on larger acts of courage, like asking people for money to fund your political campaign and taking the stage in political debates.

Ultimately, those small acts of courage move you toward what you've been working to achieve all along: hitting your desired target, where it's time to shine—no matter what pops up to throw you for a loop.

The Courage To Dance With What You're Given

You're speaking at a prestigious event, a target you've spent three months preparing for.

As you stride confidently across the low stage, the audience of 300 business professionals gobbles up your words like a gourmet meal. *I'm on fire,* you think, *I'm a speaking goddess!* In a haze of glory, you take two steps forward toward your adoring audience, and neglect to notice that you have run out of stage. In one slow, horrifying moment, you pitch headlong onto the dirty hotel carpet floor, a tumble of arms, legs, and high heels. To make matters worse, a videographer is three feet away, videotaping your graceless fall for posterity.

Awful, huh?

Well, yes it was. I was the speaker who fell off the stage. And while I was unhurt (at least physically), it was jarring, and not a little embarrassing.

I bring up this awkward moment as proof that when the curtain literally or metaphorically goes up and you step into your spotlight moment, anything can happen. Though you may not fall dramatically off the stage as I did, you might be asked a question you can't answer, get harsh pushback from a colleague on data you've shared, or spill your coffee all over your laptop and kill your lecture notes.

There's no denying that the take a risk phase involves stepping into high-stakes situations where unexpected challenges abound. It's like taking a ballroom dancing class, where you're expected to dance with an ever-changing assortment of partners. Some of them are nimble and graceful, and a joy to twirl with. Others are foot-stomping klutzes, struggling to lead or be led. Either way, you have a choice: play small and retreat, or go with the flow and dance with the partner you're given.

To go with the flow, you need to be able to bring yourself to a place of center, breathing, and relaxation, because you can't think, risk, or speak effectively in a body that's locked down by fear (or "sphinctered up," as I like to say). That's why it's so important to have self-soothing, centering practices in place to help you regain control and recover your wits when something goes awry in a critical spotlight moment.

Reset And Recover With F.B.I.

Remember F.B.I., (Foot, Breath, Intention), the three-step R & R & R preparation tool I use regularly when I'm on deck waiting to speak (and that I teach all of my clients)? It also happens to be one of the best recovery practices I know. Think of it as a life preserver you can grab onto when you're thrown for a loop in a conversation or presentation and feel vulnerable or uncertain.

To use F.B.I. as a recovery tool, you need to have a bottle of water handy and do the following:

First, *find the floor with your feet*. Pull yourself out of your head, where Moe and Schmoe are assaulting you, and get back into your body. Root yourself.

Second, *bring your breath into your belly*. As you root yourself, grab a glass of water, or your water bottle. Take a slug. Now exhale (something you automatically do after you take a drink) and regain control of your breath. Breathe in and out slowly three times.

Finally, *remember your intention*—what you're there to do—and get on with it.

Yes, it's a simple process. But simple is good, especially when your adrenaline kicks in and you have brain fog.

F.B.I. can help you recover your equilibrium and get back on track. It achieves this by helping you slow down the moment and, perhaps most importantly, slow down your breathing. As mental skills coach Bob Tewksbury writes, "Slow down your breathing and everything else seems to slow down. And when things slow down, you have a greater capacity to think and act in the moment."

I know it works, because I used F.B.I. to recover from the squirm-worthy public moment I described earlier when I tumbled ingloriously off the stage in front of my horrified audience.

But first, I laughed. And when I laughed, my audience laughed. With me. Not at me.

"I'm okay," I said, lifting myself up carefully from the floor. "Nothing's broken!"

The audience let out a collective sigh of relief. Because, after all, how you react to what happens in front of an audience helps them know how to react.

"Alrighty," I said. "Let's try this again, shall we?"

Then I stepped back onto the stage, found the floor with my feet, brought my breath into my belly, remembered what I was there to do on behalf of my audience, and got on with it.

And if my audience had been engaged with me before, they were twice as engaged with me now. Why? Because I had been willing to be very present, very human, and very imperfect in front of them. I'd also been willing to find the funny in the situation. Which helped them relate to me even more deeply.

That's the beauty and the gift of take a risk. It builds a bridge between you and your audience of one or many that makes for the kind of real moments that create indelible memories and lasting relationships.

Cultivate A Daily Practice Of Presence

As with anything, the more you practice dropping your cloak of invisibility and taking the risk to be present, the easier it gets. And the more you can claim the stage with lasting impact and influence.

So, cultivate a practice of presence by practicing being present as often as you can, in and out of spotlight moments.

Practice sharing and revealing your true feelings, needs, and desires with family members, coworkers, and even the stranger ringing up your groceries at the store. For example, instead of simmering in angry silence, try telling your spouse that you're hurt or angry around a specific behavior. Or say no to an activity with a friend that you really don't want to engage in.

Practice telling personal stories and anecdotes that build a bridge with your listener, even if it initially feels awkward.

Practice staying uncovered and being honest in tough conversations, even if what you are revealing is not perfect or pretty.

Practice using F.B.I. as both a preparation and recovery tool, so it becomes easier for you to determine and return to your place of peace, center, and safety.

Then go take a risk to reveal yourself when you claim the stage in the bigger, high-stakes spotlight moments you've been aiming for:

Shock the heck out of your colleagues on the executive team by dropping your coat of invisibility and speaking up boldly and often at your monthly C.F.O. meeting.

Fire up your audience and potential constituents with your words, passion, and authenticity when you accept your nomination for public office.

Speak candidly and confidently to your boss about why you're ready for a promotion and greater responsibility as a leader.

Say no, and mean no, when you're asked to do something you neither want to do nor need to do.

Deliver your presentation at the business pitch competition in such a compelling, human, and relatable manner that your audience of potential investors can't wait to talk to you and support your service, product, or big idea.

Remember that sometimes vulnerability can be your biggest asset. *So, reveal, don't conceal.* Take the risk to be present and real, so you make a real difference in the spotlight.

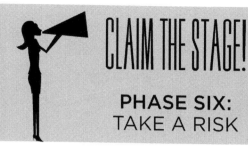

PHASE SIX:
TAKE A RISK

Reveal yourself. Be willing to drop your cloak of invisibility and let people really see and hear the real you, warts and all. This means letting go of the need to be perfect and opening yourself up to being vulnerable.

Engage in small acts of everyday courage. Take the risk to speak up and share your wisdom, even when it feels scary. Find the courage to ask for what you need, even if you think it might rock the boat. Dare to share your true feelings, even if you're worried it might upset someone else. Remember, courage is like a muscle. The more you work it, the stronger it gets.

Dance with what you're given. When things go wrong in a spotlight scenario, be willing to turn lemons into lemonade. Laugh, breathe, recover, and open your arms wide to the joy of being human and fallible in front of an audience that is also human and fallible. Then get back up and keep going.

Try F.B.I. Reset and recover by grounding yourself (foot), bringing your breath into your belly (breath), and reminding yourself of the task at hand (intention).

Practice being present. As with anything, the more you practice revealing yourself to others and being fully in the moment, the easier it gets.

Take A Bow

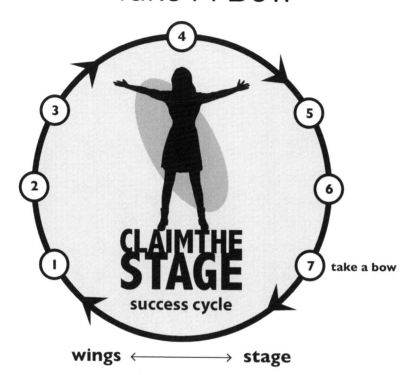

wings ⟷ **stage**

*You get whatever accomplishment you're
willing to declare.*

—GEORGIA O'KEEFE, AMERICAN ARTIST (1887-1986)

It was our final coaching meeting. Serena, a top-level sales
professional with a wry, dry manner, was kicked back in her chair
giving me a play-by-play of the pivotal sales presentation she had
successfully given that morning.

"I was so ready, you know?" she said with a chuckle. "I mean, we'd worked on it for two months, right? I could have done that presentation in my sleep. I did my preparation rituals and routines while I was waiting to start the sales pitch and felt really relaxed and centered. And when it was time, I stepped in front of the client—the CEO, the VP, the head of marketing were all there—and started to talk. And it just flowed. From the moment I started, to the moment I ended, I knew I had them. Whenever they asked me a question, I just took a breath, recentered myself, and answered it, like a tennis pro swatting back lobs from an amateur. Bam! Bam! Bam! No sweat, no worries! After the Q & A, they took a break and had a huddle—that's when I texted you saying I'd knocked the pitch out of the park, remember? Then they came back in and said the contract was ours. My boss is beyond thrilled, I'm beyond thrilled, and honestly, it couldn't have gone any better."

"I'm beyond thrilled for you, too," I said. "But I'm not surprised. You worked hard to make this sales presentation the success that it was. Congratulations!"

"Thanks," she said. "I couldn't be happier. And now, I'm going to go celebrate by taking the rest of the afternoon off and pampering myself a bit. I made an appointment at a spa for a for head-to-toe treatment!"

"You deserve it. Enjoy every moment!" I said, giving her a hug and ushering her out the door. As I watched Serena drive away, I felt great joy for her. Not just because she had taken the stage so successfully, but that she was so willing to take time to acknowledge and savor her success. In so doing, Serena had completed the seventh phase of the Claim the Stage Cycle: *take a bow*.

Take A Bow: The Seventh And Final Phase Of The Claim The Stage Cycle

Take a bow, which is the final phase of the Claim the Stage Cycle, directly reflects my background as a professional actress. It underscores the fact that, in the theater, the performance of a play is not officially over until the actors return to the stage to take a staged and rehearsed bow while the audience applauds. When actors take a bow, they give themselves space and time to savor what they've just completed. They take a well-deserved moment to bask in the appreciation expressed by the audience's applause, as well as in their own feelings of triumph, joy, and satisfaction at having taken the stage to the best of their abilities.

A stage play would feel incomplete to both the audience and the actors without the curtain call. After all, applause is a gift, and you'd never refuse a gift. The same holds true when it comes to the successful completion of any important project or goal. Giving yourself time and space to take a bow and savor your success before moving on to the next task down the pike marks a definitive conclusion, like a period at the end of a sentence. In addition, it builds confidence, boosts self-worth, and allows time for rest and renewal before the next round of challenges.

That said, I can't tell you how many of my clients are hell-bent on skipping right over the final take a bow phase so they can focus on whatever is next on their journey. Which is exactly what happened with my client, Dior.

Dior's Story: "Don't Make Me Go There!"

Dior was a very capable, forty-something expert in safety and compliance whose discomfort with advocating for herself had kept her stuck in a dissatisfying, lower-level position for too long. "I'm tired of just *doing*," she declared at our first meeting "I want to be *influencing*."

Numerous sessions and a few months later, Dior burst onto our Zoom coaching call with big news:

"Oh my God!" she said. "My boss offered me a team lead position! A team lead, which could potentially tip into a management position! I can't believe it! I honestly don't know what to do with myself right now!"

"You're finally moving toward management," I said. "This is wonderful news!"

"Yeah," Dior continued with barely a breath and her brow furrowing. "There are a few caveats though: We haven't completely worked out the money, I'll have to wait six months until being considered for a full managerial position, I have to hit certain benchmarks along the way, and…"

"Dior," I said, raising my hand, "hold on a second."

She stopped in midsentence, eyebrows quirked, clearly surprised at my interruption.

"Before you gallop ahead to what's next, I'd like to strongly suggest that you take a breath and take a moment to acknowledge what you've accomplished and where you are right now."

"Yes, but…" she stammered.

"The buts can wait a little, Dior. I assure you that all the details in your new position will eventually be ironed out. But right now, I want to remind you of just how far you've come since we started our work together:

"First, you *took stock* of where you felt stuck and stopped as a potential leader. Then, you *took ownership* of your blessings, and of the internal and external blocks that were holding you back from embracing and expressing your worth. Next, you *took aim* by clarifying the goal you wanted to reach, which was an increased ability to speak up and advocate for yourself so you could be seen as a leader and move toward a managerial position. Then, you *took steps* to make that goal a reality by examining and reframing your limiting beliefs and behaviors, speaking up more in meetings, scheduling an appointment with your boss to explain your readiness for a role with more responsibility, and role-playing with me what you'd say to her. Then you *took your cue* by not backing off from attending that meeting, even though I know you were anxious about it. And once you stepped into the meeting, you *took the risk* of speaking honestly to your boss about what you needed and wanted. Which ultimately persuaded your boss to offer you a better position. You did all of that, Dior!"

'I guess that's basically true," Dior said grudgingly. "I did do all those things. But I couldn't have done them without you."

"Dior," I said, "I may have been there to counsel you during our meetings or suggest techniques and methodologies, but you were the one who did the tough, inner work. You were the one who practiced the concepts I taught you, in meetings and in conversations. You made all this happen."

"You probably say that to all your clients," Dior said, the corners of her mouth turning up just a little. "And besides, I only did what I had to do."

"I don't give praise unless praise is due. You've earned my praise, and you've earned the right to praise yourself."

"Saying good things about myself is hard to do," Dior said, avoiding my eyes and squirming in her seat. "You know I don't like going there."

"I know it makes you uncomfortable," I pressed on, "and that's precisely why I'm making you do it." I smiled. "And, by the way, you may not like 'going there,' but 'going there' is exactly what you did when you talked to your boss. Which, in terms of our work, is a cause for major celebration. Because even if nothing had come out of it, even if you hadn't been offered a great, new position, you hit the target you'd been aiming for: You found the courage to speak up boldly for yourself and express your desire for a greater leadership opportunity. Which, by the way, means you've now completed six of the seven phases of the Claim the Stage Cycle."

Dior thought for a moment. "You're right," she finally agreed, her shoulders relaxing and her smile brightening. "I spoke up in ways I never would have before you and I started meeting. And because I did, my boss offered me a job that's going to open the door to a management level position. And I'm going to have the freedom to build and lead a big team and make decisions, which is what I've always wanted. And my boss even said she would mentor me through the transition process and help me learn the ropes as a leader. I mean it just doesn't get any better, right?"

Suddenly, Dior launched into a seated, wiggly, happy dance. "*I'm awesome!*" she yelled, pumping her fists and giggling like a kid.

"You certainly are," I said, giggling, too, "and I'm disgustingly proud of you!"

"Me, too," she said, with a gigantic grin, still dancing away.

"Hey, Dior," I said, leaning toward the screen. "Do you know what you just did?"

She shook her head.

"You took a bow. Which means you just completed the seventh phase of the Claim the Stage Cycle. Congratulations, not only on the job offer, but for taking the time to acknowledge a job well done!"

And then I joined Dior in her wiggly, giggly happy dance, pleased to be celebrating such a gratifying and well-earned conclusion to our months-long coaching engagement.

Making Peace With The Pause For Applause

There's nothing I like better than witnessing or sharing in a client's take-a-bow moment, whether it comes in the form of a triumphant text ("I knocked my presentation out of the park!"), an exultant email, or a detailed debrief in context of a coaching session. Some clients struggle, however, to give themselves permission to savor their success. In Dior's case, though it might have taken awhile to get there, she was finally willing to pause for applause (from me, and from herself) and to acknowledge the hard work that had led her to a triumphant accomplishment. Knowing her proclivity to play small and diminish her worth, I wasn't terribly surprised that she would have preferred to avoid taking a bow and shining a light on her accomplishments. She, like many of my clients, just doesn't like "going there," because "going there" means having to wade into the murky middle of discomfort.

It bears pointing out that this discomfort with "tooting your own horn," "boasting," or "shameless self-promotion," as I have often heard my clients somewhat disparagingly term it, is a running theme for many of my clients during the entirety of the Claim the Stage Cycle. Though it's especially prevalent in the take a bow phase, it often shows up during phase two of the cycle (take ownership) when I ask a coaching client to read their list of blessings (talents, abilities, positive qualities, gifts) to me. "Do I have to?" they ask, twisting in their chairs like a punished child, "It's just so *hard!*" And when I invite a woman to read her list of blessings to a group, the discomfort ratchets up even higher. I distinctly remember the look of horror on the face of an attendee at one of my *Stop Playing Small* workshops when I asked her to stand up and read her list of blessings to the eighty or so women in the room. "Can I tell you my friend Sandra's blessings instead?" she blurted, pointing to her neighbor. "She's *really* accomplished!"

Angie, a middle-aged researcher who was struggling to be promoted to a position of higher leadership at the university where she worked, perfectly expressed this resistance to "tooting her own horn" when she confessed, "I struggle with promoting myself. It makes me uncomfortable. It's a lot easier for me to promote other people. But if I don't learn to promote myself, I'm not going to get a promotion—here or anywhere."

Acknowledging one's accomplishments (especially to someone else) can be hard for women to do because we've been raised to believe that it's immodest to take credit for our accomplishments.

Which is why, like the woman at my workshop who didn't want to share her list of blessings, many women would rather praise someone else than "brag" by shining a light on themselves.

As communication coach Peggy Klaus writes in her book *Brag! The Art of Tooting Your Own Horn Without Blowing It*, "It's a well-researched fact that women are terrible self-promoters. Told by parents and society at large 'Don't be a show-off,' 'Don't upstage your brother,' 'Don't talk about your accomplishments—it will make your boyfriend/husband look bad,' women are less likely to draw attention to themselves and take ownership of their successes. They tend to attribute their accomplishment to other people, their families, or a work team. That's all very nice, but it's those who visibly take credit for accomplishments who are rewarded with promotions and gem assignments."[21]

In her groundbreaking book *Reviving Ophelia*, clinical psychologist Mary Pipher explains that women learned to be self-effacing to a fault as adolescent girls in middle school. She describes middle school as the place where "girls first learn to be nice instead of honest," and when they receive "rigorous training for the female role. At this time," Pipher writes, "girls are expected to sacrifice the parts of themselves that our culture considers masculine on the altar of social acceptability and to shrink their souls down to a petite size. Claudia Bepko and Joann Kresan [authors of *Too Good For Her Own Good*] call it 'indoctrination into the code of goodness.'"[22]

In middle school, fitting in is more important than standing out, tending to one's relationships is preferable to tending to one's own needs, and the accusation of "You're so conceited" slaps girls down into shame and silence. In class, an adolescent girl might opt to be quiet and make light of her intellectual abilities rather than risk being called a "brain" or a "showoff." Bestselling author Alice Hoffman captures this tendency poignantly and perfectly in her novel *Practical Magic*, in a passage describing what Sally, a young girl, chose to do to fit in at her new school:

> *She tried not to be noticed. She pretended she wasn't smart and never raised her hand in class. She disguised her own nature so well that after a while she grew uncertain of her own abilities. By then, she was quiet as a mouse. When she opened her mouth in the classroom, she could only squeak out wrong answers; in time she made sure to sit in the back of the room, and to keep her mouth firmly shut.*[23]

This choice to stay quiet and to publicly minimize their abilities is internalized and carried forward as girls grow into adulthood and step into the professional workplace, which is why many bright, capable women tend to sit and wait for someone else to notice them and their accomplishments. As Linda Babcock and Sara Laschever observe in their book *Women Don't Ask*, women will often put in a great deal of effort toward doing the work and being deserving, all the while hoping or assuming that someone else will eventually pay attention and reward them.[24] And when, despite their hard work and the metaphorical gold stars they've collected along the way, their boss or colleague doesn't consider them for a position or make them the offer they expect, they are utterly bewildered.

According to research by Women of Influence and Thomson Reuters, women hold hard to the belief that their achievements will somehow miraculously speak for themselves. The study also found that self-promotion (as in tooting your own horn, bragging, or whatever else you want to call it) is the second biggest pitfall for women in business, mitigating their career advancement.[25]

Men, on the other hand, apparently have far less compunction about bragging. And bragging gets them noticed and promoted. Shonda Rhimes, the creator, head writer, and producer of the massively popular television series *Grey's Anatomy*, *Private Practice*, and *Scandal* highlighted the discrepancy in self-promotion between men and women in a speech at Elle magazine's *Women In Hollywood* event in October 2018. "Women do not brag enough," she said. "…men brag and women hide." Then she proudly declared, "I will not hide. I am the highest paid showrunner on television." And then she admitted that, even for her, making that statement publicly was hard to do.[26]

The fact is, hiding by diminishing your abilities or accomplishments because you've been led to believe it's not nice or because it's not polite only serves to keep you small and out of the spotlight. As award-winning author, speaker, thought leader, and recent United States presidential candidate, Marianne Williamson, wrote in her book *A Return to Love: Reflections on the Principles of A Course in Miracles,* "Your playing small does not serve the world. There is nothing enlightening about shrinking so that other people won't feel insecure around you."[27]

Learning to say thank you when praised, instead of "it was nothing" is an important step for many women. Learning to say "I'm proud of my efforts" or "Here's what I've accomplished and what I'm capable of" is important, too, if you want to stand out and more effectively claim the stage and step into positions of greater leadership. If it helps you be more willing to do it, think of the pause for applause as a gift—a gift to yourself, or a gift from others. And you would certainly never refuse a gift.

There's another extremely important reason for you to be willing and able to take a bow: Every time you do it, you're modeling behavior that just might be noted and copied by your daughters, or other younger women in your office who are looking to you for leadership. This point was driven home hard after survey respondent Amy Matthews, a director of sales at a global food service company, chose not to tell her twin five-year-old girls about her promotion to management in an effort to be humble "and not brag." When she took an after-hours call, her girls complained and asked why she had to answer the phone. "Because I am the boss," she replied, "and sometimes my team needs me to help them." "Girls aren't bosses!" one of her girls exclaimed. Amy was horrified, realizing that by downplaying her accomplishments she had contributed to her girls' beliefs that women couldn't be leaders. "Now," she writes, "I make it a point to celebrate my own wins to my kids so they know they can do and be anything."

By celebrating and sharing your accomplishments, you strengthen your "going there" muscle. Simply put, by humbly practicing "tooting your own horn" you become a better horn tooter, which will certainly help you improve your ability to claim the stage and, ultimately, take a bow.

To Take A Bow Better, Practice

As every actor knows, learning how to gracefully take a literal bow takes practice. The same holds true for learning how to take a metaphorical bow. The more willing you are to acknowledge your accomplishments and your greatness (and make no mistake, there is greatness in you), the easier it will become for you to gracefully savor and share your success.

Practicing pausing for praise and self-celebration can be particularly difficult for those of us with type-A personalities who are driven to go-go-go with little room to reflect, play, or breathe. And so we downplay and gloss over our accomplishments, soldiering on to the next project or task through which to prove our worth. I say "we" because, quite frankly, this has been a lifetime struggle for me, too. As the daughter of parents who praised effort and accomplishment, and who lifted their eyebrows at a B+ on my report card instead of focusing on all the As, I have been driven to move without pause (or praise) from one accomplishment to another. Over the years I have had to consciously train myself to stop and take a bow and savor the moment after a job well done instead of saying or thinking "That was nothing! On to the next big thing!"

How I Learned To Take A Bow

The first time I remember consciously taking a bow and slowing down to savor my success occurred when I was twenty-five and understudying the leading role of Polly Peachum in a production of

The Threepenny Opera at the famed Guthrie Theater in Minneapolis. One night, twenty minutes before the curtain was to rise, I was suddenly called to take the place of the actress playing Polly, who was too sick to go on.

Simply having been cast in the show was already a huge accomplishment for me, since it marked my debut as a paid professional, card-carrying union actress. But having to take the stage in a top-of-the-line production in front of a packed house in a role I'd only ever rehearsed once on the theater set (and never in costume with the rest of the cast and the full orchestra), was a serious challenge. I flung myself into it with every part of my being. And when I took my bow at the end of the show, I was exultant. I had done it! I had come through, with little formal rehearsal and under extreme pressure. And, as I discovered, I had apparently been good enough to fool an accomplished visiting theater director in the audience into thinking he'd been watching the experienced Julliard-trained actress listed in the program who was supposed to have been playing the part.

I remember how exhilarated and satisfied I felt afterward, knowing in my gut that I had taken the stage with fire and flair. To make things even sweeter, once the curtain fell, my fellow cast members hugged me, kissed me, gave me a massive handmade card filled with congratulatory wishes, and celebrated my performance with an impromptu party.

These kind gestures only added to my soaring sense of joy and accomplishment. The next day, to further commemorate this milestone accomplishment, I went to the Guthrie's gift shop and bought myself a gorgeous pair of earrings that are still one of my most cherished possessions.

Over the years, I've continued this practice of symbolically taking a bow by buying myself a small memento to commemorate big achievements like giving a keynote at a major event or picking up the initial batch of copies of my first book, *Touch the Sky*. And if I don't buy myself a memento as a way to take a bow, I celebrate by having a great meal with friends or family, where we toast my accomplishment with gusto.

Taking a bow and savoring your success is certainly easier to do when you're happy with the outcome that taking the stage has brought you. But what if the thing you've worked toward doesn't manifest the way you'd hoped?

Taking A Bow When You Have To Bow Out

Sometimes what you hoped to gain from claiming the stage doesn't materialize, no matter how well you performed. Someone else wins the election, is offered the consulting contract, gets the book publishing deal, or gets the acting role you went after with all your heart.

The latter happened to me too many times to mention when I was auditioning for roles in plays, movies, and TV shows in New York and Los Angeles. I'd pin all my hopes on a role that I just *knew* was meant for me, go through a series of challenging auditions and callbacks, get down to the nail-biting wire ("It's just between you and one other woman," my agent would say. "But they love you, they really do!") and then, for whatever reason (I was too tall, they wanted a blonde, I didn't have enough experience, they cast the producer's daughter, blah blah blah), I wouldn't get the part. The loss was devastating every single time, and in direct proportion to the amount of work I'd put into claiming the stage in my auditions.

Was it easy for me to take a bow and congratulate myself for a job well done in the face of that kind of deep loss and disappointment? Was it easy for me to take a bow when I was forced to bow out from something I wanted with every part of my being and had worked hard to achieve?

Heck, no.

But once the sting had subsided, I learned to reflect on the fact that I'd done the best I could and gotten pretty darn close in an ultracompetitive business. And over time, I learned to take a bow in celebration of the courage, gumption, talent, and perseverance that had put me in the running for the role in the first place.

That said, there's no question that, when you've claimed the stage with all you've got and you don't achieve your desired outcome, it can be harder to take a bow. In this case, before you can move on to seeing and celebrating all the good that came from your efforts (and there is always good to celebrate), you need to give yourself time and space to explore your feelings of frustration, sadness, or disappointment. You need to pause to mourn or mull over what didn't go your way or as well as you expected.

And then, you need to take a breath and acknowledge how brave, bold, and beautiful you are for having chosen to step into the Claim the Stage Cycle to begin with. Because unlike many others who stay hovering in the wings hidden under their cloak of invisibility, you chose to step into the game, the arena, the spotlight, with courage and intention. You put in time, effort, heart, and hope. You gave it all you had. And so even if the outcome wasn't what you expected, you absolutely deserve to take a bow—maybe even more so than if the outcome had been more to your liking.

Whether the outcome from claiming the stage is or isn't what you'd hoped to achieve, there is always something to celebrate and learn from your journey through the seven phases of the Claim the Stage Cycle. You've just got to be willing to pause for a take-a-bow moment of self-reflection.

To encourage this sort of positive, postperformance self-assessment, I'd like to share with you a simple tool I developed that I call The Four Questions.

The Four Questions: A Simple Postperformance Evaluation Tool

I created The Four Questions as a way for my clients to evaluate themselves after claiming the stage in critical spotlight moments like giving an important talk, leading a critical meeting, or engaging in a job interview. The Four Questions reflect the postperformance methodology that my master-level acting teachers and directors engaged in with me in order to help me review and analyze my work so I could develop myself fully as an actress.

Though The Four Questions are intended for self-reflection, they're also a great way to guide feedback from a trusted source, like a coach, good friend, or business colleague. I typically ask my coaching clients The Four Questions when they have tipped into the final phase of the Claim the Stage Cycle, and we are debriefing the spotlight moment they have worked toward, and finally, completed.

Here are The Four Questions (and yes, asking them in numerical order is the way to go):

1. Did I honor my intention?

2. What went better than I expected?

3. What didn't go as well as I'd hoped?

4. What might I do differently the next time?

The first question is designed to get you to focus on what you were ultimately there to do in service to your audience of one or many, which presupposes that you've claimed the stage in your spotlight moment with a clear understanding of your intention, or purpose.

The second question nudges you to find something to celebrate, and around which to take a bow. The reason this question comes up second in the list is to counteract the tendency to immediately leap toward question number three and roll around in what didn't go so well. It's deeply important that you open yourself up to seeing and feeling whatever positives you can find in your claim-the-stage experience. This is what builds confidence, which builds presence, which builds power.

The third question gives you time and space to look at what might have tripped you up or gotten in your way. It's not designed to make you feel bad in any way. It's designed to help you see what beliefs or behaviors might still need work so you can continue to learn and grow as a leader, speaker, and influencer.

The fourth and final question is the one that gets you to look ahead toward further growth and development—because, when it comes to mastery, there is always something to learn and do to move you to the next level.

The Four Questions are another form of ritual, routine, and repetition that you engage in after, instead of before, you claim the stage. They give you a structured, methodical way to assess your performance. They can keep you from going down the rabbit hole of self-flagellation that too often beckons after you've completed your time in the spotlight. And they can encourage you to pause for praise and take a well-deserved bow.

Make It A Habit To Take A Bow

If you choose, The Four Questions can become a great habit to engage in as you complete each Claim the Stage Cycle that you step into and complete throughout your life.

Because, as I will remind you in our final chapter, once one Claim the Stage Cycle ends, another will eventually and invariably begin. And you want to be ready for it.

So before you step into the next cycle, *take a pause for applause.* Remember that applause is a gift of appreciation, and you don't want to refuse a gift—especially one that can help you step into the next Claim the Stage Cycle with renewed confidence, focus, and vigor.

PHASE SEVEN:
TAKE A BOW

Pause for praise (self and otherwise). Be willing to stop and savor your success before you race off toward another project or goal. This allows you to both put a period on the Claim the Stage Cycle you've completed and honor all the time, effort, and heart you've put into it.

Practice taking a bow. Be willing to "go there," to stop and savor your success and to engage in self-praise (or praise from others), again and again. The more you do, the easier it gets.

Reward yourself. Acknowledge the take a bow phase (which is also the end of the Claim the Stage Cycle) by treating yourself to something nice. What activity or special purchase might please you and mark the occasion?

Ask yourself The Four Questions. Whether or not the outcome of your efforts was what you intended, there is always something to celebrate and learn from. Get into the habit of asking yourself The Four Questions after the conclusion of a Claim the Stage Cycle, and after every critical spotlight moment.

CHAPTER 10

Use Your Words To Change Your World

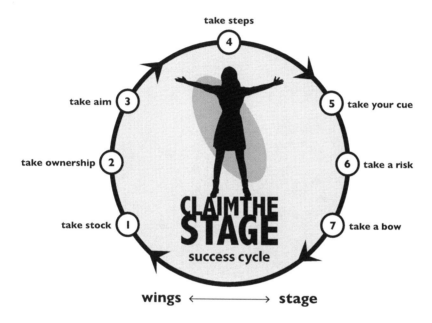

We are all meant to shine…And as we let our own light shine, we unconsciously give other people permission to do the same.

—MARIANNE WILLIAMSON

The work is behind you. You have successfully navigated each of the seven steps of the Claim the Stage Cycle.

You have taken a moment (or two, or three) to luxuriate in a well-earned bow. You have enjoyed the sweet satisfaction that comes from having seen something you cared deeply about through to completion.

That said, here's something to contemplate: In the bow you have just taken, a seed is growing. The seed of your next Claim the Stage Cycle. Because that's how it works. Cycle follows cycle, in an ever-unfolding series of cycles. There will be new, higher-stake targets to hit, new opportunities with greater visibility in which you can shine and spread your wisdom, with even greater impact and opportunity. Embracing cycle after cycle of change and expansion is how you grow as a person, and how you develop mastery as a speaker, communicator, and leader.

When you've finished a cycle, and you're ready for the next one, you'll know it. You'll hear the whisper—*could be more!*—in your heart and soul. You'll find yourself at the beginning of a cycle again, taking stock of where you are in relation to where you want to go.

If, for example, you've hit your target of speaking locally to a small group, maybe you'll now feel compelled to up the stakes and speak at a national conference. If you've successfully run for city council, maybe you'll begin to consider running for a position at the state level. If you've reached the level of sales manager, maybe you'll begin to feel the itch to rise to the position of director of sales. If you've starred in college theater productions, maybe you'll start to wonder, as I did, *What if I move to New York City to audition for Off-Broadway and Broadway plays?*

The dissatisfaction with where you are will eventually propel you into moving forward toward the next cycle. And once that next cycle is complete, there will be another cycle beckoning you forward, nudging you toward further spotlight moments in which you can have more reach, visibility, and impact.

The never-ending chain of Claim the Stage cycles is like the laundry: You wash, dry, fold, and put away a large load. And it feels so good, that completion, the neat drawers of freshly laundered undies, the clean jeans stacked on the shelf. But then, danged if the laundry doesn't pile up again, faster than you'd think possible. Suddenly, you're all out of socks and underwear, and your kid desperately needs his soccer shirt, which is at the bottom of the laundry basket. And so you lumber into the laundry room carrying a massive pile of dirty clothes and go through the whole process again. That's what it's like with the Claim the Stage cycles that you step into, one after the other, in your continual quest to claim the next stage, and the next stage, and the next stage.

Now, you may be thinking: *Jeez, cycle after cycle after cycle, ad nauseum? That sounds exhausting! I'd rather have another margarita and keep celebrating my last Claim the Stage Cycle!*

To that I say, go ahead and have that margarita. Get a massage. Take a nice little rest and recover your energies. You certainly deserve it. But then, once you're feeling rested and ready, stay alert for the inner nudge toward the next stage.

Because it will come. Maybe you'll run across a job posting for a next-level position that not only makes you recognize how dissatisfied you are with your current job, but also how much you're longing for greater leadership opportunities. Or maybe a colleague will suggest you give a talk at an upcoming conference, and your soul cries, "Yes! Do it!" even as your fear of public speaking says, "Are you crazy?" The point is, the nudge toward another cycle will come, whether you want it to or not.

And maybe you'll respond to that nudge by thinking *I stepped into the cycle before, went through all the phases, and it didn't pan out. Why should I step back in and try again?"*

Or maybe the nudge will come, and you'll think, "I'm kind of okay where I am, sort of in and out of the wings. Why bother stepping back into the cycle?"

Why bother? I'm so glad you asked.

From The Fire, Reborn

It was 1998, and I was living in Los Angeles, in the thick of my new career as a singer and songwriter. I remember it was eleven o'clock in the morning on St. Patrick's Day. I was still in my jammies when the computer screen imploded. BAM! Just like that.

What the hell?

Then I smelled it: *Smoke! I smelled smoke!*

Fire! My apartment was on fire!

"Get the cat, get Cassie!" I yelled to my husband. "I'll call the fire department!"

But the cat wouldn't come out from under the bed.

And the fire department went to the wrong address. It took them forever to get there.

And the smoke got so bad, we had to leave our things behind, our home behind, our two-year-old cat, Cassie, behind.

My husband and I stood on the sidewalk and watched the flames climb higher and higher and get hotter and hotter.

And we held each other. Sobbing, screaming. *Cassie! Cassie!*

Finally, the fire department managed to put out the flames. And a burly firefighter finally, finally brought Cassie to me. She was tiny in his arms, her head bouncing limply in time to his steps.

Two firefighters—angels, both of them—tried to resuscitate Cassie by sliding a mini oxygen mask on her muzzle and performing CPR. But she was gone.

And the apartment? Toast. Uninhabitable.

Miraculously, the one room that was untouched by the fire was what I called my music room. My piano, my guitars, the hard copies of my original songs, and the boxes containing 1,000 newly minted copies of my first CD, *I Will Fly*, were all unscathed.

This seemed ironic, considering the last thing I felt like doing was singing, or making music.

Amid my shock, my sorrow, my mourning, I remembered: *Oh, God! I have a concert to give in two days!*

And I could have canceled it, right? I mean, I had a great excuse, the person who had booked me would have certainly understood.

But you know, I'm a professional performer. The show must go on, the songs must be shared, and all that.

So two days later, I strapped on my guitar and drove to the performance venue. When it was time, I stepped onto the stage, feeling like a raw, gaping wound. I let myself speak from my heart, sing from my soul. I let the audience in on what had happened, not for their pity, but because I felt it was right that they know, and I couldn't not share it.

And my songs? Well, they took on new meaning, new depth, as I sang them. I revealed myself to my audience in ways I never had before. And when the tears came, I just took a breath, let it be, and kept on going.

It was a tough, vulnerable, brave, and necessary night.

The audience applauded. And I took my guitar and went home—well, home to my friend's spare bedroom—exhausted.

In the morning, I checked my email. There was a message from someone I'll call Scott.

"Eleni," he wrote. "You don't know me. I'm a performance poet. And I've been very depressed. Suicidal, in fact. Last night, I had planned on going home and ending things. But as I was walking by a coffee house, I heard you singing, and your voice pulled me through the door. The more you sang, the more compelled I felt to stay and listen. And as I watched you up on that stage, so publicly in your grief, so willing to genuinely share yourself with your audience, I thought *If Eleni can keep going through the hell she's just been through, then so can I.* So thank you, for literally saving my life."

And as if his email wasn't enough to help me understand why getting on that stage and sharing my songs, my heart, and my experience mattered, he added one more thing: a beautiful poem he'd written especially for me.

To this day, Scott's poem is one of my most precious possessions, and a symbol of one of the most important lessons I've ever learned: You never know whose lives you might change for the better, when you bravely step onto the speaking platform, into the meeting, into the conversation and share your message, your big idea, your vision, your wisdom with your audience of one or many. That's why, when the inner nudge does come, I hope you'll straighten your back, open your arms wide, and stride forward yet again into the first step of yet another Claim the Stage Cycle. And, near the end of that cycle, when you step from the wings and into the spotlight, know and trust that the words you speak might be exactly what someone in your audience needs to hear.

So drop your coat of invisibility and dare to Claim the Stage, over, and over again. Find the courage to share who you are and what you know on public platforms large and small.

And remember what my mother told me: *Sometimes you just have to say something.*

Say what you have to say, when you need to say it. Say it with confidence, courage, and conviction. Say it because if you don't, who will?

Just say it.

Because you matter.

Your words matter.

Use your words to change your world.

Stop That, Start This: Ten Habits To Break Or Build So You Can Be Seen And Heard As A Woman of Power (Especially By Men)

1. **Stop** putting yourself or your accomplishments down ("It was nothing," "This is probably a silly question"). **Start** acknowledging praise or accomplishment with a simple "Thank you."

2. **Stop** apologizing (incessantly) for things you didn't do or that are out of your control. **Start** apologizing (sincerely) only when you are in error.

3. **Stop** undermining yourself with tag questions ("The movie was great, don't you think?") or by using qualifiers or hedgers ("I think," "I feel," or "sort of") that imply a lack of confidence in what you're saying or a need for affirmation. **Start** speaking with conviction, in a declarative manner: "This movie kept me riveted from the opening credits."

4. **Stop** nodding and smiling continuously like a little bobble-headed doll, which can be misunderstood as agreement. **Start** practicing keeping a neutral expression when someone is speaking and nod and smile only when you definitely agree.

5. **Stop** speaking in a teeny, tiny voice when what you have to say matters. **Start** risking speaking up and being heard, even if it makes you uncomfortable.

6. **Stop** beating around the bush. **Start** getting to the point and sticking to the point, even if you're dying to elaborate.

7. **Stop** adding words *after* you've made your point, which can imply uncertainty. **Start** trusting that what you've already said is enough and doesn't need endless elaboration for it to matter more.

8. **Stop** initiating a conversation when you're highly emotional. **Start** taking a moment to sort out your feelings and get clear on what you want to say and why you want to say it before engaging in a difficult conversation.

9. **Stop** robbing yourself of your power by slouching or stooping. **Start** sitting or standing like a queen, with your head upright, shoulders back and your body relaxed as you survey your domain.

10. **Stop** minimizing your physical presence by standing or sitting in demure, restricted stances that imply shyness or a lack of self-confidence (e.g., crossing your arms, hands, and legs like pretzels, standing with your feet pinned together). **Start** taking ownership of the space around you with energized, focused movements and a planted, rooted stance (like a beautiful oak tree).

APPENDIX B

Coaches, Consultants, Trainers

Karen Andrews: An award-winning HR professional who can give you advice on what to do if you've been sexually harassed at work. www.karenandrewsgroup.com

Judy Ravin: Owner of www.lessaccents.com, which has tools and techniques to help you minimize a heavy accent so you can be understood more clearly.

ZingTrain: Visioning workshops, leadership training, among other great resources. www.zingtrain.com

Minal Sampat: Social media and marketing expert who can help you expand your reach. www.minalsampat.com

Lesley Everett: Branding expert and coach who can help you solidify your personal and professional brand. www.walkingtall.com

Mark LeBlanc: A business development expert and coach who can help you take your business to the next level. www.growingyourbusiness.com

Carrie Hensel: Website and written content developer par excellence. www.colorhivecreative.com

Henry DeVries: Author and owner of Indie Books International, who can help you start, finish, and market the book you need to write, so you can up your visibility as an expert and get bigger speaking engagements. www.indiebooksintl.com

Suggested Reading List

Brag! The Art of Tooting Your Own Horn Without Blowing It, Peggy Klaus

Be a Better Leader and Managing Ourselves, Ari Weinzweig

Claim the Stage! Workbook, Eleni Kelakos

Claiming Your Place at the Table, Brooke Warner

Defining You, Mark LeBlanc, Kathy McAfee, and Henry DeVries

Down, Girl: The Logic of Misogyny, Kate Manne

Growing Your Business, Mark LeBlanc

Navigate: The Five Types of People and Pick! Choose to Create a Life You Love, Sherene McHenry

Never Be The Same, Mark Le Blanc

Positive Strategies for Change, Linda Babcock and Sara Laschever

Reviving Ophelia: Saving the Selves of Adolescent Girls, Mary Pipher

Shrill: Notes From a Loud Woman, Lindy West

So People Say You're an Asshole, Sarah Brabbs

The Artist's Way, Julia Cameron

The Charisma Myth, Olivia Fox Cabane

The Confidence Code, Katty Kay and Claire Shipman

The Courage Code, Megan Raphael and Jennifer Byron

The Desire Map: A Guide to Creating Goals with Soul, Danielle LaPorte

The Firestarter Sessions, Danielle LaPorte

The Gifts of Imperfection and *Dare to Lead,* Brené Brown

The War of Art, Stephen Pressfield

Touch the Sky: Find Your Voice, Speak Your Truth, Make Your Mark, Eleni Kelakos

Women & Power, Mary Beard

Women Don't Ask: The High Cost of Avoiding Negotiation, Linda Babcock and Sara Laschever

Writing Down the Bones, Natalie Goldberg

Acknowledgments

This book would not have been born without the support of numerous midwives and doulas along the way.

First and foremost, I am beyond grateful to the women who took the time to fill out the surveys that informed the contents of both this book and the accompanying *Claim the Stage! Workbook*. Thank you for trusting me with your fears, hopes, and dreams. I wrote this book for you, and for the hundreds of coaching clients I've worked with for almost two decades who have trusted me to steer them toward their most empowered, genuine selves.

Deep appreciation to my book coach, editor, and brother-from-another-mother, Henry DeVries of Indie Books International. You understood the premise of this book from the get-go, and turned yourself inside-out to snip, shape, and support my words so that they said what I needed them to say. And a resounding thanks to Vikki and Devin and all the members of my Indie Books family whose expertise and advocacy brought this book into being.

Many thanks to Morgan Stanfield, who started the journey with me as my initial book coach. I so appreciate your belief in me, your deep wisdom, and your help creating the surveys that shaped this book.

To Mark LeBlanc, my years-long business coach and dear friend, thank you for reminding me "You can always take another step."

Much gratitude to Marty Somberg of Somberg Design for creating the Claim the Stage Cycle graphic that kicks off many of the chapters. It's yet another example of the great work you've produced for me over nearly two decades of collaboration.

To Sherene McHenry, PhD, The People IQ expert, thank you for your wise counsel and precious friendship. Without you there would be no *take your cue* phase of the Claim the Stage Cycle.

And speaking of counsel, heartfelt thanks to my forever friend Amy Albert for the nuggets of insight, mined from the rich soil of your dual perspective as writer and psychotherapist.

A huge, love-drenched thank you to my mastermind sisters, Karen Jacobsen and Lesley Everett, who were at my side (at a retreat, in pjs, goblets of wine in hand) when I declared I was going to write this book. Thank you for lovingly nudging me to complete it, and for always helping me feel sane and loved.

To my sis-in-law, Katy Fleming, thank you for cheering me on and for modeling how to walk in the world as an actualized woman unafraid to speak her truth.

I'd also like to pay tribute to a group of women who have contributed mightily toward my own commitment to share my voice and elevate others: Virginia Giordano, music producer, visual artist and activist whose perpetual enthusiasm for my work always spurred me forward; Lisa Michelson, powerhouse singer and actress, whose abrupt passing (so long ago and way too soon) kicked off my work as a singer and songwriter; my resourceful grandmother, Vasiliki Plakias, who never met an obstacle she couldn't cheerfully overcome; Dorothy Fleming, my spunky mother-in-law, who was never afraid to say what she felt; my cousin, Martha Tsiros, who always spoke her mind and never shirked the work needed to achieve mastery; and my mother, Theresa Plakias Kelakos, whose huge, artistic spirit and passionate advocacy always made me feel like there was absolutely nothing I couldn't achieve. Though these remarkable women may have left the Earth plane, their vibrant spirits stir my soul daily.

I couldn't have completed this book without the rock-solid support of my husband, Jim Fleming, aka Zen Boy. Thank you for helping me find space and inspiration to write by insisting that we convert our storage area into my Magic Room. My love for you is an always thing, and I am forever grateful for the little yellow taxi we were destined to share that sparked our passionate partnership.

About The Author

Eleni Kelakos, The Speaker Whisperer®, is president of The Eleni Group, founded in 2003. She uses performance techniques learned over twenty years as a professional actress in New York and Los Angeles to help executives across the globe be more impactful and relatable when they give presentations.

When she's not coaching individuals, or facilitating trainings at companies like General Motors, Allstate, and Kubota Tractors, Eleni practices what she preaches, empowering people with her signature keynote presentations at conferences nationwide.

An award-winning, nationally touring singer-songwriter, Eleni has produced and recorded four acclaimed music CDs: *I Will Fly*, *To the Bone*, *Where I Come From*, and *Touch the Sky!* Her songs have been featured in the film *Dispossessed* and danced to by *America's Got Talent* semifinalist Beth Ann Robinson. And she's sung the national anthem at Shea Stadium for three (winning!) Mets games.

A graduate in both theatre arts and semiotics from Brown University, Eleni is a past president of the Michigan chapter of the National Speakers Association. Her book *Touch the Sky: Find Your Voice, Speak Your Truth, Make Your Mark* was a gold medal winner of the 2014 Global Ebook Awards. She lives happily with her husband, Jim, and two constantly shedding cats, in Ann Arbor, Michigan.

For more about Eleni, visit www.theelenigroup.com. To hire Eleni as a speaker or coach, write to eleni@theelenigroup.com or call 734-622-0522.

[APPENDIX F]

Works Referenced

1   Molly Wood, "Partners in the Service: Foreign Service Wives a Century Ago," American Foreign Service Association, *The Foreign Service Journal*, June 2020, http://www.afsa.org/partners-service-foreign-service-wives-century-ago.

2   Connie Glaser, *GenderTalk Works: 7 Steps for Cracking the Gender Code at Work*, (New York, NY: Windsor Hall Press 2nd ed., 2011), p.19 and 34.

3   Mary Beard, *Women in Power: A Manifesto,* (New York, NY: Liveright, 2017).

4   "The 2019 State of Women-Owned Business Report," commissioned by American Express and prepared by Ventureneer. https://s1.q4cdn.com/692158879/files/doc_library/file/2019-state-of-women-owned-businesses-report.pdf.

5   Hillary Rodham Clinton, *What Happened,* (New York, NY: Simon & Schuster, 2017).

6   Abigail Lambert, "Could Hillary Clinton's Voice Cost Her The White House?" *Pacific Standard* magazine, May 3, 2017, https://psmag.com/news/could-hillary-clintons-voice-cost-her-the-white-house.

7   James C. Collins, *Good to Great: Why Some Companies Make the Leap… and Others Don't,* (New York, NY: Collins, 2009).

8   Arianna Huffington, *Thrive: The Third Metric for Redefining Success and Creating a Life of Well-Being, Wisdom, and Wonder,* (New York, NY: Crown, 2014).

9   Hal Elrod, *The Miracle Morning: The Not-So-Obvious Secret Guaranteed to Transform Your Life (Before 8AM),* (The Miracle Morning Publisher, 2012).

10   Elrod. *The Miracle Morning.*

11 Danielle LaPorte, *The Desire Map: A Guide To Creating Goals With Soul,* (Boulder, CO: Sounds True Inc., 2014), p. 36.

12 Ari Weinzweig, *A Lapsed Anarchist's Approach to Managing Ourselves,* (Ann Arbor, MI: Zingerman's Press, 2013).

13 Carmine Gallo, "3 Daily Habits of Peak Performers, According to Michael Phelps' Coach," Forbes.com, May 24, 2016, https://www.forbes.com/sites/carminegallo/2016/05/24/3-daily-habits-of-peak-performers-according-to-michael-phelps-coach/#4c658b77102c.

14 Lynn Stuart Parramore, "Trump's '60 Minutes' Interview Underscores America's Ongoing Manterrupter Problem," NBCNewsNow.com, October 6, 2020, https://www.nbcnews.com/think/opinion/trump-s-60-minutes-interview-underscores-america-s-ongoing-manterrupter-ncna1244707.

15 Bob Tewksbury and Scott Miller, *Ninety Percent Mental: An All-Star Player Turned Mental Skills Coach Reveals the Hidden Game of Baseball,* (New York, NY: Hachette, 2018), p. 107-108.

16 Tewksbury and Miller. *Ninety Percent Mental.*

17 Michelle King, "Jacinda Arden, New Zealand Prime Minister's Message To Women: Be Yourself, It's Good Enough," Forbes.com, November 28, 2017, https://www.forbes.com/sites/michelleking/2017/11/28/jacinda-ardern-new-zealand-prime-ministers-message-to-women-be-yourself-its-good-enough/?sh=fe8e52732b93.

18 Greg McKeown, *Essentialism: The Disciplined Pursuit of Less,* (New York, NY; Crown, 2014).

19 Neesha Arter, "Tony Award Tastemakers: What's Your Pre-Show Ritual?", Observer.com, June 6, 2015, https://observer.com/2015/06/tastemakers-whats-your-pre-show-ritual/.

20 Megan Raphael and Jennifer Byron, *The Courage Code: It's Yours. Break it. Own it. Use it.,* (Traverse City, MI: Utopia Press, 2006).

21 Peggy Klaus, *Brag! The Art of Tooting Your Own Horn Without Blowing It.* (New York, NY: Warner, 2003), p. xviii.

22 Mary Pipher, *Reviving Ophelia: Saving the Selves of Adolescent Girls.* (New York, NY: Ballantine, 1994), p. 39.

Also quoted from this book is a reference to a quote from Claudia Bepko and Jo-Ann Krestan. *Too Good for Her Own Good,* (New York, NY: HarperCollins, 1990).

23 Alice Hoffman, *Practical Magic,* (London: Scribner, 2017).

24 Linda Babcock and Sara Laschever, *Women Don't Ask,* (New York, NY: Bantam, 2007).

25 Rebecca Horan, "Stop Being So Modest! Why Women in Business Need to Get Comfortable with Bragging." Entrepreneur.com, January 18, 2019, https://www.entrepreneur.com/article/326531.

26 Chloe Hall, "Shonda Rhimes 'Brags' That She's The 'Highest Paid Showrunner In TV'. Now It's Your Turn," October 16, 2018, https://www.elle.com/culture/a23813828/shonda-rhimes-elle-women-hollywood-speech/.

27 Marianne Williamson, *Return to Love: Reflection on the Principles of A Course in Miracles,* (New York, NY: HarperCollins, 1992).

**Take a deeper dive into the Claim
the Stage Cycle with the**

Claim The Stage!
Workbook:
The Unabridged
"Director's Cut"

It's chockful of additional material, research,
worksheets, and exercises to help you move with clarity
and focus from the wings to the spotlight.

Learn more at www.theelenigroup.com

Made in the USA
Middletown, DE
20 February 2022

61412273R00102